CAREERS IN THE

SECRET SERVICE

BY ADAM WOOG

Cavendish
Square

New York

Published in 2014 by Cavendish Square Publishing, LLC
303 Park Avenue South, Suite 1247, New York, NY 10010

This publication represents the opinions and views of the author based on his or her personal experience, knowledge, and research. The information in this book serves as a general guide only. The author and publisher have used their best efforts in preparing this book and disclaim liability rising directly or indirectly from the use and application of this book.

CPSIA Compliance Information: Batch #WW14CSQ

All websites were available and accurate when this book was sent to press.

Library of Congress Cataloging-in-Publication Data
Woog, Adam, 1953-
Careers in the Secret Service / Adam Woog.
p. cm. — (Law and order jobs)
Includes bibliographical references and index.
Summary: "Provides a comprehensive look at the careers available in the Secret Service"—Provided by publisher.
ISBN 978-1-62712-434-8 (hardcover) ISBN 978-1-62712-435-5 (paperback) ISBN 978-1-62712-436-2 (ebook)
1. United States. Secret Service—Juvenile literature. 2. Secret service—Vocational guidance—United States—Juvenile literature. 3. Law enforcement—Vocational guidance—United States—Juvenile literature. 1. Title.
HV8144.S43W66 2014
363.28'302373—dc23
2011030884

EDITOR: JEFFREY TALBOT   DESIGNER: JOSEPH MACRI
PHOTO RESEARCHER: MARY BETH KAVANAUGH
PRODUCTION MANAGER: JENNIFER RYDER-TALBOT   PRODUCTION EDITOR: ANDREW CODDINGTON

CAREERS IN THE

SECRET SERVICE

CONTENTS

INTRUCTION

IT WAS EARLY AFTERNOON ON MARCH 30, 1981. JUST two months into his first term, President Ronald Reagan stepped outside the Hilton Hotel in Washington, D.C., where he had just made a speech. Reagan smiled and waved at the crowd that had gathered there. They were hoping to catch a glimpse of the new commander in chief.

He was flanked by a group of unsmiling men who were dressed in dark suits and were ceaselessly scanning the crowd. They were, of course, special agents of the U.S. Secret Service (USSS). Their job was to protect Reagan at any cost.

Standing in the front row, behind a barrier, was John Hinckley Jr. Hinckley was a mentally ill man who had an obsession with actress Jody Foster. He wanted to do something that he thought would get her attention.

So Hinckley produced a gun and fired six times toward the president in less than two seconds.

Special Agent Timothy McCarthy immediately threw himself in front of Reagan and was shot in the abdomen. Reagan's press secretary, James Brady, and Washington D.C. police officer Thomas Delahanty were also hit. Meanwhile, Special Agent Jerry Parr, who was leading the group protecting

The Secret Service had to take control of a chaotic situation quickly when John Hinckley Jr. attempted to assassinate President Ronald Reagan in March 1981.

Reagan, pushed the president into the waiting limousine and threw himself on top of him as the car sped off.

At first, it seemed as though the president had not been injured. There were no obvious bullet wounds. But Reagan complained that his chest hurt, and Parr could see that there was frothy blood coming from the president's mouth when he breathed.

So Parr made an important decision. He could have directed the special agent driving the car to return to the White House, which had its own medical facilities and was extremely secure. But Parr decided that it would be better to risk reduced security in favor of getting Reagan to a hospital that had experts in trauma cases.

It was a good move. A bullet had ricocheted off the limousine and struck the president under one arm. It had lodged in his left lung, near his heart. Reagan would probably have died if not for the immediate actions of Parr and his colleagues. In an interview with PBS, *Washington Post* reporter Del Quentin Wilber, who was there, commented about Parr,

> "His quick actions got Reagan out of Hinckley's direct fire and behind the shielded limousine door. . . . And the president's life— literally, Ronald Reagan's life came down to a split-second decision by Jerry Parr and one inch, because that's how far the bullet was from his heart."

As always, the Secret Service had made sure that all nearby hospitals would be prepared to handle a presidential emergency. Standard procedure for the agency is to make sure beforehand that nearby hospitals are secure, that teams of special agents are already on site, and that doctors are standing by and ready for just such an emergency. The surgeons were successful in removing the bullet, and Reagan made a full recovery. The other officials who had been shot also survived, although Brady was severely wounded and suffered permanent brain damage.

HIDDEN WORK

It goes without saying that an attack—even an unsuccessful one—on the president or another dignitary protected by the USSS would have profound, even world-shaking consequences. Fortunately, such events are extremely rare. The men and woman employed by the Secret Service are very good at their jobs of making sure everything goes right, and they are well aware that the stakes are always high. In 2009, Secret Service Director Mark Sullivan commented, "We understand the historic significance. If we make a mistake, it's going to be devastating for the country. We're not going to let the country down."

Working on the Secret Service's protective detail is, to say the least, an exceptionally stressful, high-pressure, and demanding job. But it is by no means the only one that you might take on if you choose a career in the Secret Service. For one thing, special agents do much more than just guard important people. Notably, they also are charged with the task of shutting down the production of counterfeit money and investigating other financial crimes.

The Secret Service wages war against illegal financial operations in a number of ways. It has specialists who analyze suspicious bills to check their authenticity. Also, many of its agents are assigned to duties such as investigating and apprehending criminals engaged in fraud, such as embezzlement (stealing money that belongs to a company you work for), or "skimming" (attaching devices in ATM machines that steal customers' information and make withdrawals).

The combination of protective duty and tracking counterfeiters may seem strange, and if not for a twist of fate, it never would have happened. The original Secret Service, created to stop **counterfeiting**, took over the protection of the president. It did this because, at the time, it was the federal agency that was most capable of the job. Some observers have pointed out that being such a hybrid is perhaps not optimal for an effective law enforcement agency. Writer Marc Ambinder notes, "It may be true that if you designed the entire national-security apparatus from scratch, investigating financial crimes would fall outside the purview of the Secret Service." Nonetheless, that is how the Secret Service evolved.

OTHER OPPORTUNITIES

Of course, being a special agent would not be your only option if you chose a career with the Secret Service. Another opportunity for employment is in its Uniformed Division. The officers in this unit are responsible for security on the grounds of the White House and at other key government buildings.

The agency also employs thousands of other people in a wide variety of positions. These men and women make up the agency's support personnel. Ranging from specialists in such fields as information technology and forensics to office staff and database managers, they provide the day-to-day work that keeps everything in the service running smoothly.

No matter what your position might be within the Secret Service, the public will see only a fraction—or perhaps none—of the work you do. Most of your job, if you're doing it right, will be hidden.

First Lady Michelle Obama summed it up this way in 2009. She was making a speech to a group of Secret Service and other federal law enforcement employees. The first lady remarked

A Secret Service detail accompanies First Lady Michelle Obama. The organization is tasked with protecting the family of the President.

[F]or many of you, your work takes place behind the scenes. The truth is that if you do your jobs well, then few people will ever know about anything that you do. For others, the hope is that you never have to execute much of what you work so hard to prepare for.

This concealment is deliberate, of course. If the Secret Service is going to carry out much of its mission, then the work must be, well, secret. But it is vitally important work, and maybe it is the career for you.

WHAT THE SECRET SERVICE DOES

SPECIAL AGENT MCCARTHY, WHO WAS WOUNDED in the attack on President Reagan, is not the only Secret Service agent who has been wounded or killed on the job. But he is the only one who has deliberately thrown himself in front of a **protectee** to, in this case literally, "take a bullet for the president."

Contrary to popular belief, special agents do not officially swear an oath to take a bullet. Rather, they are prepared to do what it takes to prevent such a situation from ever happening. As one agent put it,

> [W]hat we'll do is we'll do everything in our power to keep the bullet out of the event. And that's what the Secret Service is all about. It's about being prepared, it's about meticulous advance preparation, and it's about training properly so that when you do your job, you don't have to bumble around for the steps that you take.

THE EARLY DAYS

The job of keeping that potential bullet out of the event may be the best known of the Secret Service's activities, but it was not the organization's original purpose. Nearly a century and a half ago, the Secret Service came into existence for one very particular reason: the federal government needed to stop the flow of counterfeit money.

In the middle of the nineteenth century, counterfeiting was a major problem. It has been estimated that at that time about a third of all the money in circulation in the U.S. was phony. In large part, this was because states, and even individual banks, could print their own bills. Since the quality and look of each institution's currency was different, it was especially easy to manufacture and use false money.

To curb the problem, in 1865 President Abraham Lincoln signed into law a bill that authorized the formation of a special federal agency. Its first official name was the Secret Service Division, and it came under the direction of the U.S. Department of the Treasury. (Today, the Secret Service is under the jurisdiction of the U.S. Department of Homeland Security (DHS), a huge umbrella agency that was formed in the wake of the 9/11 terrorist attacks. The DHS oversees many of the nation's law enforcement and security organizations.)

In a strange twist of fate, the date on which Lincoln signed the papers that officially created the Secret Service was July 5, 1865. That evening, John Wilkes Booth, a Southerner who was bitter about the direction of the Civil War, assassinated Lincoln as he watched a play at Ford's Theater.

The murder was not just a tragedy—it was a tragedy that

could have been avoided. The Washington, D.C. policeman assigned to guard the entrance to the presidential box, John Frederick Parker, had left his post to catch a glimpse of the play. Then, during the play's intermission, he and Lincoln's footman and coachman went to a nearby tavern, giving Booth the opportunity to sneak into the president's box and shoot him in the back of the head.

THE SECRET SERVICE TAKES ON PROTECTION DUTY

In the wake of President Lincoln's assassination, government authorities realized that in the future all presidents would need more serious security around them. At first, the U.S. Marshals Service took over this duty. The main reason for this was that the Marshals Service was one of the few federal law enforcement agencies in existence at the time. Many of today's major law enforcement agencies, such as the Federal Bureau of Investigation (FBI), had not yet been established.

Meanwhile, the USSS was proving to be very resourceful at its job of stopping counterfeiters. Within two years of the service's formation, the *Philadelphia Telegram* newspaper was able to dramatically declare the Secret Service's effectiveness in this pursuit: "The chase is as relentless as death, and only death or capture ends it."

But it was not until 1894 that the Secret Service became involved in any protection duty. Even then, it maintained only a small, informal contingent of special agents at the White House. President Grover Cleveland and his family were then

BREAKING A
COUNTERFEIT RING

New York, Miami, and Los Angeles are favorite locations for counterfeiters. On average $100,000 in fake currency is detected every week in the Los Angeles area alone. So Secret Service agents in these cities are constantly tracking down and dismantling counterfeiting rings.

For example, the service busted an operation in North Hollywood that had already passed $700,000 in phony bills. It was discovered after local police officers stopped a car for a traffic violation. They found an envelope on the front seat stuffed with $20 bills. They were so freshly printed that there was still green ink smudged on the envelope.

The driver was only a minor part of a network of twenty-five people, including printers, middlemen, and passers. Secret Service agents traced the network back to the young criminal behind it. He had been using Mac laptops to print the counterfeit bills. Special Agent Brian Hunter, who directed the operation that caught him, commented, "This gentleman was about as good as they come in the reproduction of the new series of notes. We always want to take the [printer] down. . . . That is the head of the snake. But usually we end up grabbing the tail first."

Source: Stefan Lovgren, "U.S. Secret Service's Other Job: Fighting Fake Money," National Geographic News, October 22, 2004, http://news.nation-algeographic.com/news/2004/10/1022_041022_tv_secret_service.html

The Secret Service first began protecting the President during the Grover Cleveland administration in the 1890s.

occupying the residence. The Secret Service began taking over protection when the service began investigating a group of **anarchists** in Colorado who had allegedly hatched a scheme to assassinate Cleveland.

As the Secret Service followed up on this plot, it was also given the assignment of protecting the president. According to the report of the Warren Commission, which was the official inquiry into the death of President Kennedy:

> Secret Service men accompanied the President and his family to their vacation home in Massachusetts; special details protected the President in Washington, on trips, and at special functions. For a time, two agents rode in a buggy behind President Cleveland's carriage, but this

Despite their vigilance, the Secret Service hasn't always been able to avoid tragedies, such as the assassination of John F. Kennedy.

practice attracted so much attention in the opposition newspapers [opposing Cleveland] that it was soon discontinued at the President's insistence.

But it was not until two more presidential assassinations occurred—James Garfield in 1881 and William McKinley in 1901—that Congress formally handed the full-time responsibility of guarding the nation's leader to the Secret Service. In his 1993 article about the history of the Secret Service, *Washington Post* reporter Joel Achenbach commented, "It took three dead presidents to get the Secret Service into the protection business."

It has been the responsibility of the Secret Service to investigate threats against and protect every president since

McKinley. For more than fifty years, there were only a few serious incidents, and none of those proved to be fatal. But then came a single, devastating event: the assassination of President John F. Kennedy in 1963.

In the wake of that tragedy, the Secret Service's presidential protective detail dramatically increased and the agency's other divisions grew proportionately. Back then, the Secret Service had about three hundred special agents. Over the following decades, the Secret Service also computerized and expanded its databases, to keep better tabs on potential threats.

Furthermore, it greatly expanded the number of agents assigned to advance protective work—that is, preparing sites prior to presidential visits—and their responsibilities. It also created counter-sniper teams to guard against potential assassins shooting rifles from a distance. Additionally, the agency greatly expanded its training facilities, and it began to coordinate its efforts with other law enforcement agencies more closely.

In short, the Secret Service became even more serious than before. According to some sources, for example, improving agents' training and other aspects of the job were long overdue. Special Agent Taylor Rudd comments, "Before the Kennedy assassination, training often consisted of agents telling war stories. Many agents on duty had never had any training."

EXPANDED DUTIES

There have been serious incidents in the decades since then, such as the attack on Reagan, but JFK's death was only the fourth successful presidential assassination in U.S. history. In large part, this is because of the Secret Service's efforts to investigate and, if necessary, arrest the people behind the death threats that all presidents receive.

Meanwhile, the Secret Service's protection duties have expanded to include a number of others besides presidents and their families. Also guarded today are key government officials, including the vice president and others who would be next in line if the president died, as well as their families. Furthermore, the service protects official representatives of the United States and their spouses when they travel on government missions abroad, as well as foreign dignitaries who are making official visits to the U.S.

For years, presidents and their families also had lifetime guards after leaving office. However, that has changed. Bill Clinton was the last president to receive such protection. Now, former presidents are guarded for only ten years after leaving office. (There are two exceptions: a president's widow or widower is protected until remarriage or death, and the children of former presidents are protected until the age of sixteen.)

The same protection is also provided for major party presidential candidates. Normally, this begins four months before an election. However, the policy was changed during the campaign leading to the election in 2008 of the nation's first African-American president. The Secret Service extended the length of time it guarded Barack Obama to about eighteen months prior to the election.

This was primarily for two reasons. First of all, the candidate's popularity meant that he drew huge gatherings of people wherever he appeared. This was coupled with the thousands of death threats—far more than the average against a presidential candidate—that Obama began to receive after he announced his candidacy.

The avalanche of threats has continued to increase since Obama was sworn into office. (The Secret Service does not say exactly how many, out of security concerns. They are afraid that discussion of threats in public might encourage more. The number of threats presidents receive in a given year has been estimated at about three thousand, and it is likely that the numbers are far greater for President Obama.) In a *New York Times* article, reporters Helene Cooper and Brian Stelter commented:

> While the question of how well the president is protected is never a casual one, it has taken on special resonance with Mr. Obama, the nation's first black president. Even when he was a candidate, his security rivaled that of a sitting president.

Even as the protection duties of the Secret Service have expanded, the organization has not forsaken its first role as an anti-counterfeiting agency. In fact, the Secret Service has taken on still more duties. Notably, today it is also intimately involved in operations designed to safeguard the nation's economic well-being, such as battling a variety of fraud operations.

Furthermore, since the terrorist attacks of 9/11, the Secret Service (along with other federal law enforcement agencies) has taken on major aspects of the nation's anti-terrorism activities. Julia Pierson, a special agent who became Chief of Staff for the Secret Service in 2008, summed up these multiple roles:

> People don't realize the investigative duties that we have. Besides counterfeiting, we investigate cyber crime and electronic access device [such as ATM] fraud. We have joint jurisdiction with the FBI for bank fraud. We're responsible for providing communications support for the president and those at the White House. We also have an intelligence group, and maintain liaisons with the military and state and local law enforcement to keep pace with any potential threats.

OFFICERS AND SUPPORT PERSONNEL

All of these varied responsibilities are, in part, carried out by the Secret Service's two main branches of **sworn officers**: its special agents and its uniformed officers. But by no means are sworn officers the only positions available within the Secret Service. In fact, hundreds of other specific jobs need to be filled in the agency's offices around the country and overseas.

These jobs, as in any law enforcement organization, form a network of employees who can support the duties of the agency's sworn officers. The men and women of the Secret Service's support staff are experts in a range of specialties, including technical, scientific, professional, investigative, and administrative roles.

THE SECRET SERVICE BY THE NUMBERS

In 2009, the Secret Service:

• Had a 100% success rate in the safe arrivals and departures of protectees

• Provided protection for 4,696 travel stops for domestic protectees and 2,182 travel stops for visiting foreigners

• Protected 189 heads of state and heads of governments, as well as their spouses, during the Sixty-fourth UN General Assembly in New York City

• Screened 4.14 million people at campaign-related events, using more than 4,500 **magnetometers**

• Retrieved and screened more than three million pieces of mail at the White House Mail Screening Facility

• Provided a total of 3,117 calendar days of protection for former presidents and their spouses, as well as 4,117 for foreign dignitaries and spouses (considering all agents on duty)

• Oversaw security for the inaugural ceremony of Barack Obama and related events, which drew an estimated 1.8 million people to Washington, D.C.

• Produced and distributed 84,472 Secret Service inaugural credentials and 12,303 vehicle placards for the inaugural events

• Screened more than one million visitors during the inaugural events

• Screened 64,750 people at preinaugural train stops

• Conducted protective security advances and other support for 390 overseas sites

• Made 2,506 domestic counterfeiting arrests, assisted in 360 foreign arrests, and helped to confiscate a total of more than $182 million in counterfeit U.S. currency

Source: FY09 Secret Service Annual Report,

While most think of the agents in suits protecting the President, the Secret Service also has uniformed officers, such as this group combing the south grounds of the White House for evidence after a 1995 incident.

Since support staffers work mainly behind the scenes, they are not as familiar to the public, or as glamorous, as special agents or officers. Nonetheless, they play vital roles in the agency's operations. In fact, the agency couldn't function without them.

Besides—how cool would it be to be able to say you work for the Secret Service, even in an entry-level position?

Some of the service's support jobs are highly specialized. Others are more typical of the kinds of jobs you'd expect to see in any large organization or company. Among these positions are those of:

- Forensic specialists, responsible for collecting and analyzing scientific evidence in crime investigations
- Psychologists, experts in anticipating and following up on the psychological aspects of cases or individuals

- Law enforcement instructors, who specialize in teaching subjects such as federal enforcement policies and procedures
- Firearms instructors, who ensure that agents and officers remain fully qualified in the use of deadly force
- Intelligence specialists, who collect and analyze information that may pertain to potential or current cases
- Information Technology (IT) specialists, responsible for creating, installing, maintaining, and operating computer systems
- Engineers, who handle various aspects of chemical, electronics, materials, civil, or mechanical engineering as they relate to agency operations
- Surveillance and communications technicians, specialists in using techniques and equipment that allow agents and officers to monitor potential crimes and keep in touch with each other during operations
- Building security officers, who patrol the physical buildings used by the Secret Service
- Mechanics and equipment maintenance crews, who keep the Secret Service's fleets of vehicles and stores of equipment in good working order
- Photographers, who perform a variety of roles when photo skills are needed in forensic, surveillance, protective survey, crime scene, and research photographic assignments
- Public relations officers, who act as liaisons communicating information to and from the public and media

• Human resources specialists, budget analysts, clerks, office personnel, accountants, and other staff who take care of the day-to-day operations of the Secret Service's facilities

A SMALL BUT IMPORTANT AGENCY

Even counting all of the combined personnel of sworn officers and support divisions, the Secret Service is very small. Today, it has only some 6,500 employees—about 3,200 special agents, roughly 1,300 uniformed officers, and about 2,000 support personnel. In fact, other federal law enforcement agencies dwarf the Secret Service. For example, the FBI has a combined total of nearly 34,000 sworn agents and support personnel.

Chief of Staff Julia Pierson feels that, in her opinion, the small size of the Secret Service has many advantages. She comments,

> We're a small agency with a large mission. Our size gives us the ability to have more personal knowledge of each other as employees. Some people call it a cult, other people call it a family, but I do think it's unique.

Given the small size of the organization, the sensitive nature of the work, and the stiff competition for specialized jobs, it's no surprise that pursuing a career in the Secret Service is not an easy process. Candidates for any position, whether as officers or support employees, must prove themselves by going through an intense selection process.

WHAT'S IN A CODE NAME?

The Secret Service gives code names to each of the prominent people it protects (as well as locations). These names are only for tradition. The Secret Service today relies on modern encryption technology to maintain security and confidentiality.

The code names are periodically changed but are often public knowledge. Exceptions to this are a few general codenames, in addition to individual names, that pass from one high-level person to the next:

President of the United States: POTUS
First Lady of the United States: FLOTUS
Vice President of the United States: VPOTUS

The Secret Service does not choose codenames. This is done by the White House Communications Agency. This group chooses names that are easily pronounced and readily understood —and often appropriate for the protectee's personal characteristics. For example, President Ronald Reagan's codename was "Rawhide" to reflect his love of horseback riding.

By tradition, the members of a family have code names that start with the same letter. For example, Reagan's wife, First Lady Nancy Reagan, was Rainbow; their children Maureen, Michael, Patti, and Ron were Rhyme, Riddler, Ribbon, and Reliant. Here are a few of the other codenames that the Secret Service has used:

President John F. Kennedy: Lancer
First Lady Jacqueline Kennedy: Lace

President Richard Nixon: Searchlight
First Lady Pat Nixon: Starlight

President Jimmy Carter: Deacon
First Lady Rosalynn Carter: Dancer

President George H. W. Bush: Timberwolf
First Lady Barbara Bush: Tranquility

President Bill Clinton: Eagle
First Lady Hillary Rodham Clinton: Evergreen

President George W. Bush: Tumbler or Trailblazer
First Lady Laura Bush: Tempo

President Barack Obama: Renegade
First Lady Michelle Obama: Renaissance
Malia Obama: Radiance
Sasha Obama: Rosebud

Needless to say, not everyone makes the grade. For example, tens of thousands of people apply yearly for jobs as agents or uniformed officers, but only a few hundred are accepted. The competition for support jobs, especially highly specialized positions such as those in forensic science or information technology, is also strong.

The service's thorough hiring process, of course, is designed to make certain that available jobs go to the top people in their fields. As the organization's website notes, "The men and women of the United States Secret Service come to the agency as the best of the best." So, if you're interested in a career with the service, and you think you have what it takes, it's time to look more closely at what's involved.

The first step in finding out more about a career with the Secret Service is to look at the agency's website: www.secretservice.gov.

TWO

JOINING THE SERVICE

THE SECRET SERVICE'S SITE WILL GIVE YOU DE-
tailed information about many of its various career oppor-
tunities. You can also use the site to find the Secret Service
office nearest to you and get in touch with a recruiter there.
He or she will be happy to speak with you about a career in the
service. For a complete list of field offices and contact information, visit www.secretservice.gov/field_offices.shtml.

Another way to get more information is to attend one of
the periodic job fairs in which the Secret Service participates,
or at one of the events the organization regularly holds at uni-
versities and colleges. As with visiting a field office, this is an
excellent way to speak with agents and recruiters who have
first-hand knowledge. A Secret Service agency job fair in 2009
drew more than three thousand candidates who sought to fill
more than one thousand positions. Agency recruiters also
participated in 370 job fairs nationwide, about one-third of
them specifically aimed at minorities.

In recent years, the Secret Service has attended job fairs that target minority candidates in order to increase the agency's diversity.

Meanwhile, you can also look at www.usajobs.gov, the official site listing all federal job openings. Searching this site will give you details (such as salary, location, and duties) of specific positions that are open at the moment.

GETTING SOME EXPERIENCE

Before you formally apply, you also might want to consider some of the ways of experiencing what life in the Secret Service will be like. A taste of how the world of law enforcement operates can be an invaluable asset when it's time to apply.

For example, one thing you can do is attend one of the many summer law enforcement academies or camps that are conducted around the country. These are typically sponsored by local law enforcement agencies, such as state troopers, county sheriffs, and city police.

Although these camps are not specifically designed for people interested in a career in the Secret Service, they are worthwhile for anyone who is thinking about becoming a law enforcement officer of any sort. Taking part in one of these programs will not only be a rewarding personal experience, but will also be a major plus when you apply for a position with the Secret Service because it will demonstrate that you are already serious about committing yourself to a law enforcement career.

A good way to get even more extensive experience is to join a national organization called the Law Enforcement Career Exploring program. This group is affiliated with the Boy Scouts of America, although it is open to both genders.

Typically, an Exploring program runs during the school year, and is geared to accommodate normal school hours and holidays. It is open to young people between the ages of fourteen and twenty. The cost of joining is minimal–typically $15-25 per year.

The Exploring program teams up with local law enforcement agencies across the country. Many federal agencies, among them the Secret Service, also participate in Exploring programs. If you become part of the program, you'll get first-hand experience and education in a range of law enforcement-related areas, including leadership techniques, interpersonal skills, marksmanship, the proper use of equipment, and procedures for dealing with emergencies. Active or retired law enforcement officials typically lead these classes and other activities. As you progress through the program, you'll also have the opportunity to take part in regional and national events such as conferences and advanced training.

Julia Pierson, the Secret Service's Chief of Staff, says that taking part in an Exploring program was how she got started on the path to her present position. She recalls,

> Initially, I got involved with the Law Enforcement Exploring program. . . . As I became more involved, first at a state and then a national level, I met some Secret Service agents. It was through this exposure to special agents that I thought this might make an interesting career.

You can find out more about Exploring programs at the site of the agency that oversees them: http://exploring.learning forlife.org/services/career-exploring/law-enforcement/.

INTERNSHIPS

And there's still another way for you to find out more before formally applying. This is to take part in one of the Secret Service's programs for student interns. During your time as an intern, Secret Service professionals will guide and mentor you, giving you first-hand experience that is directly related to your career goals.

As part of protecting the president, uniformed officers of the Secret Service constantly patrol the White House.

There are three basic categories of student intern programs: the Student Career Experience Program (SCEP), the Student Temporary Employment Program (STEP), and the Student Volunteer Program (SVP). Much of the work you'll do will be clerical, but even so you'll have a chance to learn the ropes and be part of a real Secret Service office. Both STEP and SCEP programs offer salaries and certain benefits, like school credit. These will differ case by case, depending on your academic record and work experience.

Completing one of these programs won't guarantee that you'll have a job when you graduate. However, you will be in a good position to apply for a permanent job. You'll have already had experience working with the Secret Service, and recruiters will already know you and the skills you can offer.

The SCEP program is designed for students specifically working toward a career in law enforcement. It does this by giving you a chance to do work that directly relates to an academic program, such as criminology. SCEP includes 640 hours of work and study, typically spread out over two school years and the summer in between. (You may be able to waive half of these hours if your GPA is 3.5 or higher.)

The STEP program is in many ways more flexible than SCEP. This is because the work you do doesn't have to relate directly to your academic goals, so you can be studying any subject and still be an intern. As with SCEP, in STEP your work will be spread out over time, typically for two school years while school is in session as well as during summer and other breaks.

Meanwhile, the Secret Service also maintains a Student Volunteer Program (SVP). As the name suggests, this internship is unpaid, but is still an opportunity to train and work with the Secret Service. If you're enrolled in the SVP program, you will be expected to work a minimum of twelve hours per week, typically for one or two semesters, two quarters, or a summer session. As with the paid student programs, being a volunteer is an excellent way to explore a career with the agency while honing your personal and professional skills.

All of these programs have certain basic requirements. You must:

- Be a U.S. citizen
- Be able to obtain a Top Secret security clearance (The Secret Service will determine this through a background check of your personal finances, criminal record, and other factors.)
- Be at least sixteen years old (or sixteen at the time of appointment)
- Be enrolled full-time as a degree-seeking student in an educational program accredited by a recognized body
- Maintain a cumulative grade point average of at least 3.0 (for STEP) or 2.5 (for SCEP and SVP)
- Get a written agreement from your school
- Be able to type at least forty words per minute (for SVP only)
- Not be a son or daughter of a current Secret Service employee

You can find out more about all of the agency's various internship programs by visiting www.secretservice.gov /opportunities_interns.shtml or the government's site for federal student internships: www.usajobs.gov/ei/studentcareer experience.asp or www.studentjobs.gov.)

THE MINIMUM YOU'LL NEED

Whether or not you take part in a summer academy, an Exploring program, or an internship, you will need to meet some basic requirements before you can apply to the Secret Service.

Of course, the details of what's needed will differ depending on the particular job you're applying for. However, there are some basic requirements that are true for all positions within the Secret Service. Notably, you must:

- Be a U.S. citizen
- Be able to pass random drug tests
- Certify you have registered with the Selective Service System if you are a male between the ages of 18 and 25, or certify you are exempt from having to do so under selective service law
- Qualify for a Top Secret clearance and undergo a complete background investigation.
- Be a high school graduate or hold a GED equivalent

Beyond these minimum requirements, each job category will have specific requirements. For example, some jobs require years of training and experience and advanced educational degrees. Obviously, someone applying for a job in, say, information technology will need to have extensive education and experience in that area. On the other hand, some jobs don't require any particular experience, and in some cases a college education is not needed.

To apply for a position as a sworn officer, in addition to the minimum requirements, you must:

- Be between the ages of twenty-one and thirty-seven (or will be at the time of appointment).

This age requirement is for special agents. The age range for applicants to the Uniformed Division is slightly different. To be a candidate for that position, you must be between twenty-one and forty (or will be at the time of your appointment).

- Possess a current valid driver's license
- Be able to pass a drug test and a polygraph test
- Have at least a bachelor's degree from an accredited college or university, and have met at least one of these requirements:
- Be in the upper third of your graduating class
- Have a college grade point average of 3.0 or higher
- A member of an accredited scholastic honor society

OR

- Have at least eighteen semester hours of graduate level education

OR

- Have at least one year of specialized experience in or directly related to the job. This educational requirement is for special agents. To apply for a position as a uniformed officer, you don't need formal education beyond having graduated from an accredited high school or earning a GED equivalent
- Be in excellent mental and physical health and overall fitness, and be prepared to undergo extensive testing in these areas. Fitness is a crucial aspect of training for the Secret Service. Only candidates who are in top physical condition will pass the physical fitness test. On the other hand, you will have ample time to prepare before you need to take it.

A RANGE OF EDUCATION AND EXPERIENCE

Contrary to what many people think, to apply for a position as a special agent or uniformed officer it's not necessary to have majored in criminal justice or another course of study directly related to law enforcement. In fact, in many ways it's better to include a variety of science, liberal arts, and other classes in your education. Furthermore, your training as a Secret Service

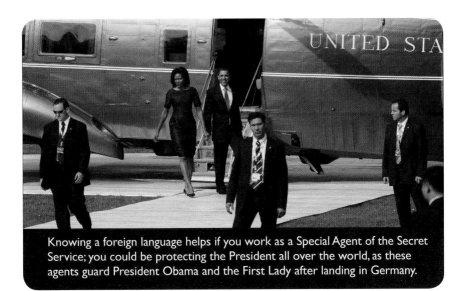

Knowing a foreign language helps if you work as a Special Agent of the Secret Service; you could be protecting the President all over the world, as these agents guard President Obama and the First Lady after landing in Germany.

agent will give you ample amount of education in the criminal justice system.

Sworn agents need to use a wide range of skills on a daily basis. A solid grounding in many different subjects is therefore best. Typically, this means some combination of science, math, computer science, writing and communication, and/or law and government. Fluency in a foreign language is especially useful, since the service protects the president on overseas trips.

You certainly don't need to have all of these—it would be a very rare person who does. But a combination of skills will certainly help. Chief of Staff Julia Pierson comments,

Whether you're an English major or studying a foreign language or getting a fitness or sports-type degree, there could be a niche for you here. You don't have to be

THE NEW YORK CITY FIELD OFFICE

A large number of the Secret Service's employees are assigned to the agency's headquarters in Washington, D.C., while others are based in some 150 field offices across the country. Naturally, the size of these agencies varies according to the needs of the region. Typically, your first assignment after you join the agency and finish your training will be to one of the service's smaller offices.

Of the agency's field offices, the New York City field office is the largest. It handles dozens of counterfeiting cases at a given time and averages six assignments a week for protective duty under normal circumstances, including spikes in activity when there are special occasions such as meetings of the United Nations General Assembly at its headquarters in that city.

Since it is the largest field office, the New York office also maintains a large cache of equipment for protective duty, counterfeit investigation, interviewing suspects and witnesses, and other activities. Among these tools are a state-of-the-art wire room, a central room for monitoring phone tracking; a vault full of items such as disguises and fake-grass tarps for agents to hide beneath when on undercover assignments; and a complex of interview rooms where special agents can conduct polygraphs and interviews, both with people connected to criminal investigations and with applicants who are candidates for the agency.

6-feet-4-inches (2 m), 300 pounds (126 kg) and built like a linebacker. We encourage agents to let us know what they want to do. We want to know their areas of interest, and we try to match them up with those kinds of assignments.

In addition to educational experience, professional experience in law enforcement, such as a few years spent on a police force, will likely enhance your chances of being accepted as a sworn officer candidate. This experience is not required. However, about 50 percent of the Secret Service's sworn agents have had previous law enforcement experience.

Other skills will definitely also affect on how your application is viewed. For example, if you are fluent in another language, or if you are skilled in a martial art, be sure to mention that on your application forms. This is one instance when it's a good idea to brag a little! On the other hand, you don't want to overdo it.

Additionally you need to be in top physical shape. Being physically fit could mean the difference between success and failure as an agent—or even the difference between life and death.

The same is true of your mental health. It's crucial, for one thing, that you remain levelheaded and quick to react in tense situations. Other aspects of mental health are just as important. For example, it is essential that you are able to work well as part of a tight-knit team. Special Agent in Charge Eric Zahren comments, "From day one, you're part of a larger mission and operate as part of a team. It's not about you as an individual."

Because of the requirement to work as a team, you must be tolerant of many different kinds of people. And you must be able to demonstrate a strong loyalty to the service and the United States.

Finally, to be a special agent, you need to be willing to go anywhere. You'll be required to sign a mobility agreement. This affirms that you are willing to be assigned to any field location in the United States, at least for your first posting. Furthermore, later in your career you might need to travel frequently and accept reassignments to offices in the United States as well as in foreign countries. (These travel commitments are not necessary for uniformed officers, since they are detailed to the Washington, D.C. office only.)

Special agent Doug Roberts notes that sometimes the travel that he and his colleagues take is pretty rustic. He remarks, "I've flown all over the world, often sitting on the floor of the plane with the cargo. It's not the most glamorous way to fly, but at least we know where our luggage is at all times."

APPLYING

If you meet these basic requirements, you can then start the application process. Again, the agency's website will lead you to the federal government's central site for job applications, usajobs.gov. Using that site, you'll be able to set up an online application customized for the particular position you are aiming for.

It's not necessary that you have access to a computer at all times in order to apply, but the agency strongly encourages it.

This is so that you can keep in touch easily during the application process. If you don't have regular access to a computer, you can contact the USSS's Personnel Division by phone at (202) 406-6090 and someone there will help you. A recruiter at your local field office can also help you work through the application process.

The first portion of the online application will ask you to provide a number of basic pieces of information—essentially, it verifies that you do meet the minimum requirements. If those check out, the service will then accept your application and the process will move forward.

The thoroughness of the process can make this is a frustratingly lengthy waiting period. For example, the process for applying to be a special agent typically takes six to nine months. (As you would expect, the timeframe and other details of the application process will be different if you are applying for other jobs.)

You will need to take part in a number of interviews, tests, and other activities during the application process. To become an agent, for example, among other things you will be attending in-person interviews, writing personal essays, and taking an increasingly tough series of written and oral exams. Furthermore, you'll have to take a drug screening test and a polygraph (lie detector) test.

The agents who are considering your application will also be looking at your overall record as a person. They'll be asking questions like: What life and work experiences have you had? Have you been involved in community and school activities

INTERNING AT THE SECRET SERVICE

While pursuing a double major in criminal justice and computer science at Central Michigan University, Bryanna Johnson had a memorable experience: she interned at the Saginaw (Michigan) Resident Office. The professor in charge of the school's criminal justice internships helped her file her application, but it was still a complex process. The background check alone took six months. Quoted in the *Central Michigan Life* newspaper, she recalls, "I had multiple interviews and I had to write sworn statements saying I had not done any drugs or illegal behavior. I had to do this in place of a polygraph test. They did a full background, and they talked to everyone I knew. They even talked to my neighbors back home that I haven't seen or talked to in a very long time."

Bryanna specifically wanted to work at a law enforcement agency that dealt with technology and computer crime, so the Secret Service was a natural fit. The agency handles much of the financial crimes that occur in the U.S., and Johnson specifically learned a lot about counterfeiting by working with agents on active counterfeiting and identity fraud cases. She stated, "I learned more in that summer than I could have ever imagined. It was a better educational experience and I learned what work in the real world is like."

The intern said that the most interesting work was sitting in on cases dealing with people who threatened protectees, she said. (Protectees are those the Secret Service protects.) This was because she interned during a presidential campaign, so many candidates came through Michigan. She met these candidates and saw how protective duty works. She even got to ride in a presidential motorcade.

Before her internship, Bryanna commented, she wasn't sure what she wanted to do as her career. After her internship, however, she knew she wanted to be a Secret Service Special Agent.

Source: Adapted from Heather Kinghorn, "Johnson interns with Secret Service," *Central Michigan Life*, February 14, 2000, http://www.cm-life.com/2001/02/14/johnson internswithsecretservice/

that indicate a commitment to others? What specific skills, such as fluency in a foreign language, will you bring to the service?

Of course, as a special agent candidate you'll also take a rigorous series of physical fitness and general health tests. However, this is not necessarily true for most support personnel positions. People with physical disabilities, for example, are clearly eligible for jobs in such fields as information technology, forensics, or linguistics if they meet the requirements. As with all federal agencies, in such cases the Secret Service does not discriminate on the basis of physical disability—or, for that matter, on the basis of sex, sexual orientation, religion, genetic information, parental status, or race.

WATCH WHAT YOU SAY AND DO!

As you proceed through the application and testing process, the Secret Service will be conducting a background investigation on you. The recruiters in charge of this will look at a variety of things, including your financial records, any police records, and your school transcripts. They will also speak to family, co-workers, and friends. The purpose is to compile a full picture of you, your character, and your strengths and weaknesses as a potential agent.

One important point to remember when planning your application to the Secret Service concerns the use of online postings. As part of your background check, the service will be looking carefully at what you have been posting on Facebook or other social networking sites, or on online discussion forums—especially those concerned with joining law enforcement agencies.

If you have posted something that would put you in a negative light, you can be sure that the service will find out about it. In fact, in some cases law enforcement agencies subpoena social networking sites, which means that they can legally require the site to give them information. So simply using a preset privacy setting will not necessarily keep your information private. The general rule of thumb, when applying to the Secret Service or any other organization, is don't post anything you wouldn't say to your parents or anyone else who might not approve of what you say.

Thousands of people apply to become Secret Service agents every year, but there are only a small number of openings. Naturally, the competition is very fierce. You will be seriously considered only if your personal history, education, and other factors are outstanding. Any serious problem, such as a felony record, will immediately disqualify you.

However, there are exceptions to these generally strict guidelines. For instance, the use of illegal drugs in your past might not automatically disqualify you for a position with the Secret Service. Applications are reviewed on an individual basis when it comes to past drug histories, so the application boards have a certain amount of discretion.

However, the agency does have general guidelines concerning past drug use. For example, one rule is that you cannot have used marijuana within three years of your application, and you cannot have been convicted of cultivating, manufacturing, distributing, processing, or selling any illegal drug.

When you go for your interview, be prepared. Be rested.

Be organized. Answer questions completely, but simply. Don't ramble on. Speak clearly and avoid slang words. Be personal but not overly friendly. Stay confident, calm, and balanced.

RECRUITING MINORITIES

The process of winnowing out the huge number of applicants to find the best ones is obviously a difficult task. Many factors go into deciding who gets chosen. Sometimes, questions of minority status become part of the consideration.

For many years, the role of Secret Service agent was reserved for men—and usually Caucasians. The first female special agents did not join the Secret Service until 1971. Barbara Riggs, the tenth woman hired as a special agent, commented,

> Yes, I encountered sexual harassment, barriers, and attitudes that women should not be law enforcement agents. There were some who did not believe women were capable, either physically or mentally, of doing the job. But I also encountered many individuals who acted as my mentors and gave me great opportunities.

Another pioneer female agent, Patricia Beckford, added, "You are always going to find a dinosaur in the bunch. You did have to prove yourself. But at a certain point, they [male agents] realized that our .357 Magnums shot as well as theirs."

Today, changes in federal laws mean that the agency is more committed to diversity than in times past. It has

While there were no female Special Agents until 1971, today the Secret Service actively recruits women for all positions.

established a number of programs specifically designed to recruit minorities and women. This is so not just for sworn officers but for support personnel as well. Among these are: conducting or participating in career fairs at schools that are largely attended by minority and female students; advertising in media sources that have diverse audiences (such as Spanish-language television); and forming partnerships with community groups and other organizations that focus on helping minorities.

Despite these efforts, however, change is coming slowly. As of 2010, only about four hundred special agents were women, out of a total of about 3,200. Furthermore, the number of ethnic minorities in the service is also fractional. As of 2010, for example, Hispanics accounted for only 6 percent of the Secret Service workforce (agents as well as support personnel).

To balance this more evenly, the agency has been making a stronger push to hire more minorities in all sections of the service. As the agency's website notes,

> We realize diversity is about more than race and gender. Diversity includes everyone, encompassing our unique differences as well as what we have in common. This is a continued agency priority that is critical to our success. . . . This allows for a strong and agile workforce while helping each individual realize their full potential.

Clearly, not everyone who applies can be hired for a given position, as a sworn officer or otherwise. But if you make it through the battery of tests, background checks, and interviews, and if you are judged fully qualified, you'll be offered a job offer, which the service calls a tentative offer (T.O.).

And if you are offered a job, you're in for an amazing experience. Not, however, before you get some training under your belt.

THREE

TRAINING

AS YOU WOULD EXPECT, THE TRAINING THAT you'll get for a job with the Secret Service will be very different depending on the position you are hired for. Many of the support jobs will be filled by people who already have the skills they need. For example, a surveillance equipment expert will already have extensive training, education, and experience in that field. If you're hired to maintain records and databases, you'll likewise already have the skills necessary for that job. In such cases, you'll likely need only a minimal amount of training before you start work. The most important things you'll need to learn in cases like this are about any rules, regulations, procedures, and policies that are specific to the Secret Service.

In other words, you'll learn how the Secret Service goes about using someone with your skills. You'll also be instructed in what can and cannot be done according to the agency's

President Bush observes the training of a sniffer dog during a visit to the Secret Service's Training Academy.

guidelines. In many cases, this training takes place largely while on the job. You'll be supervised and mentored by a senior employee, who will make sure you understand and can perform everything to the Secret Service's high standards.

TRAINING FOR AGENTS AND OFFICERS

But a relatively simple course of on-the-job training is not the case if you are going to be a special agent or a uniformed officer. If you've landed one of these select jobs, you and your fellow classmates will first go through two rigorous courses of study and preparation before you even start work.

Naturally, these will not be easy. They will test you and your classmates (usually about twenty-five) to the furthest reaches of your abilities. Furthermore, failure to graduate from either of the training's two parts—on the first try—will result in immediate dismissal from the program. There are no second chances when it comes to something as important as being a sworn Secret Service officer. *Washington Post* writer Laura Blumenfeld comments, "Not all of [the students] will make it. If they fail, they will leave humiliated. If they pass, they'll become members of an elite, stealthy service."

The first leg of the training period will be about three months of intensive work at the Federal Law Enforcement Training Center (FLETC) in Glynco, Georgia. This facility is operated by the U.S. Department of Homeland Security.

FLETC (pronounced flet-see) covers about 1,600 acres (645 hectare) of land. Its buildings and training facilities include sleeping dormitories, a total of eighteen firearms ranges, and a dining hall capable of producing four thousand meals a day, as well as an explosives range, a driving course, and a "neighborhood" of thirty-four mock buildings used for hands-on exercises in areas such as surveillance.

FLETC acts as a training facility for a number of other federal agencies in addition to the Secret Service, as well as for other law enforcement professionals from around the country. In fact, the general courses that you will take there are essentially the same as those taken by other law enforcement professionals. They form a curriculum called the Criminal Investigator Training Program (CITP).

The CITP course of study is a mixture of lectures, laboratories, practical exercises, hands-on training, and tests. Some

SCANNING THE CROWDS

As part of your training to be a special agent, you'll learn to spot certain details in a crowd that might tip you off to danger. Broadly speaking, agents learn to watch for unusual behavior. Former special agent William Albracht comments, "We look for a guy wearing an overcoat on a warm day. A guy not wearing an overcoat on a cold day. A guy with hands in his pockets. A guy carrying a bag. Anybody that is overenthusiastic, or not enthusiastic. Anybody that stands out, or is constantly looking around. You're looking at the eyes and most importantly the hands. Because where those hands go is key."

Source:Ronald Kessler, *In the President's Secret Service.* New York, Crown, 2009, p. 84

of the CITP classes will take place in the classroom. They will give you a general background in such areas as criminal law, report writing, and investigative procedures. You will also learn about such topics as social issues, psychology, and ethics, as well as interviewing techniques, leadership skills, and establishing contact between law enforcement agencies and citizens.

Meanwhile, much of your training will take place outside the classroom. This part of the work focuses on giving you and your classmates a wide range of hands-on experiences. Among these will be maintaining physical fitness, firearms training and certification, one-on-one defensive tactics and advanced driving techniques, suspect apprehension, and procedures for search and seizure.

As you would expect, the instructors at Glynco are seasoned experts in their fields. They typically are current or retired federal law enforcement officers or civilian experts, such as lawyers with law enforcement and courtroom experience. They'll act as both teachers and mentors in guiding you through the program. All of the work at Glynco, as well as the other training programs you will attend, will directly relate to your future job. Nothing is done just to do it, and even the most innocuous-sounding training course has a purpose.

For example, there's the training in swimming that you'll get, even if you're already a strong swimmer. You won't just be becoming a better swimmer. You'll also be practicing maneuvers that could help in some pretty unusual situations—for example, escaping from a helicopter that has crashed in the ocean while you still have your seat belt on.

It's all preventive. That is, the training will prepare you ahead of time for any situation. If you're lucky, you'll never have to use your knowledge. If there is an emergency, however, you'll know how to handle it. One of the instructors, Bobbie McDonald, comments, "Everything we teach out here, we hope we never have to do."

ADVANCED TRAINING

When sworn officers in training have graduated from the course at Glynco, they'll be ready for advanced training. This segment of your studies will last for a little over four months for agents in training, and about three months for officers in training.

What you learn and practice at this point will build on the basics you have received at Glynco. However, the courses now will be especially tailored to prepare you for your future as a member of the Secret Service. This type of training is called agency-specific training.

During your advanced training, you'll be stationed at the Secret Service's own academy, the James J. Rowley Training Center. This facility covers some five hundred acres (202.3 hectares) of land near Beltsville, Maryland.

Rowley is in an unmarked location, hidden in the woods and protected behind barbed wire and other forms of security. As it is at Glynco, the campus is home to a variety of facilities such as dorms, eating halls, classrooms, gyms, indoor and

INVESTIGATING THREATS

Much of what agents and support staff employees do involves following up on death threats. Public figures receive hundreds of death threats each year. Most are empty menaces, but some become reality, notably the killing of President John F. Kennedy and unsuccessful attacks on Presidents Ronald Reagan, Bill Clinton, and both Bushes.

Not all threats are specifically to presidents. Some are just on any public figure. Occasionally, they will direct their frustration and anger at the president if they can't get satisfaction with a lower-ranking authority.

For example, the Secret Service once handled the case of a man (identified as H. J.) who for years was tormented by what he thought were voices from government satellites. He went to Washington, D.C., believing that killing any high-level government official would stop the torment. Fortunately, the Secret Service was able to find him before he could do any harm.

The Secret Service must take all threats seriously, whether they are genuinely dangerous or not. So the service constantly finds ways to improve its ability to spot real risk. One effort was to have its forensic psychology section conduct a study, the Exceptional Case Study Project. The hope was to discover patterns among people who are possible threats.

It examined the mental states and personal histories of all eighty-three people who killed or tried to kill a public figure in the United States between 1949 and 1996. One of their findings was that they typically were people who had led very ordinary lives but were often frustrated in their ambitions. They were not monstrous, self-sacrificing, or calculating instruments of diabolical conspiracies.

Also, nearly half had recently experienced abrupt life changes, such as loss of job, marriage or health failures, or the death of a loved one. In the wake of these devastating changes, the assailants declined mentally and focused on single, consuming obsessions.

When training to join the Secret Service, recruits receive extensive firearms training.

outdoor firing ranges, a track for practicing defensive driving techniques, and buildings used for a variety of other purposes, such as swimming pools and K-9 (canine) training facilities.

As was true in the CITP, much of your time at the Rowley Training Center will be spent in classroom learning, studying specialized subjects such as techniques for investigating, preventing, and stopping cyber crime and credit card fraud; detecting counterfeit money; and emergency medicine. These studies will augment and advance what you have already learned at Glynco.

Many different techniques are used in the teaching process, from 3D video simulations to a virtual gaming system called "Tiny Town"—a scale-model array of computer-simulated buildings, roads, and other features. Agents-in-training use Tiny Town to plan, in detail, such operations as a dignitary's entire itinerary or public appearance.

The Secret Service is also experimenting with computer models for exploring in the classroom such issues as the health effects and crowd behaviors that could result from a chemical, radiological, or biological attack. Exercises like this one will help the service better prepare sworn officers to react quickly to real-life incidents.

At Rowley, you'll also put in long hours learning advanced hand-to-hand combat techniques. In simulated encounters, former agent Tim McCarthy comments, "you're attacked with guns and knives, then observed and graded on how you react." And you'll practice other tasks such as assembling, disassembling, and firing the USSS's standard-issue firearms. (As of 2011, these were SIG Sauer P229 pistols or FN Five-seven pistols.) Furthermore, you'll become proficient with other weapons such as shotguns, submachine guns, and machine pistols. Accuracy is paramount: you'll be expected to score at least 80 percent in marksmanship. You don't need to have had firearms experience already. In fact, the Secret Service prefers that trainees come without any prior knowledge. This gives the agency a chance to train them properly.

You'll also learn to use the Secret Service's many other forms of equipment and technology. This includes high tech radios, surveillance gear, and laptops with encrypted communications ability.

A major feature of the Rowley Training Center is its own version of the kind of mock town found at the Glynco facility and at other law enforcement training centers. It consists of houses, cafés, and other buildings, such as a tattoo parlor, restaurant, hardware store—even a mock airport. Classes there typically use role-playing—that is, students and professional actors pretend to be assailants trying to attack protectees.

In some respects, this mock town looks like a regular town. On the other hand, it's a regular town that might randomly be struck by an explosion—rocking, say, the pizzeria where the president is enjoying a slice. Or it may be that, out of the blue, a group of gunmen storms the church where the first lady is attending services. *Washington Post* writer Laura Blumenfeld comments, "Behind every mailbox, lamppost, and flowering bush, a killer possibly squats, racking his AK. Or, he might spray a vial of [poison] sarin."

The practice scenarios are as close to the real thing as possible. A.T. Smith, an assistant director at the center, comments, "We train unlike any other federal agency. We train to the edge, and then we lean over. . . . Our goal is to make it [reacting to situations] instinct."

You might find yourself in a mock suicide bomber vest, for example, or wearing robes because you are pretending to be a pope who is visiting the United States. Or you might zip yourself into a hazardous waste or chemical-weapons protective suit, finding out how to adjust your gas mask—but only after you've helped another student, "the president," to put his own mask on. (As part of your chemical weapons training, you'll also be exposed briefly to real gas fumes, so that you can identify the symptoms of gas poisoning if necessary.)

Not everything you learn will be so dramatic, however. For example, you'll pick up a number of mundane but useful tricks of the trade. Some of these will be common sense: don't drink liquids before going on duty, so you won't need to take bathroom breaks. If there's an emergency, yell loud—so loud that, in the pithy words of instructor Steve Mixon, "[D]ope dealers two blocks away should be flushing toilets."

Other tricks of the trade will require paying attention to small details that might easily go unnoticed. An instructor who once was the driver for President George W. Bush teaches his students, "Don't forget to lock the back doors. Nothing more embarrassing than the president busting your chops because you forgot to lock the door."

You'll even learn how to deliver a baby, in case that's necessary while you're on position. Don't laugh—it's happened more than once. In short, pay attention to the small stuff, and be ready for the unexpected. Instructor Mixon tells his students,

> Details! Think details! What is your job? The man in the most powerful office in the world—you're standing next to him with a loaded gun. . . .
>
> Use the force necessary. You can hit them with your car, stab them with a big pin. We in the Secret Service are super Type-A personalities, people who want to take control and win at all costs. [But] don't get that little extra shot in there, that extra revenge. . . .

THE K9 CORPS

In 1975 the Secret Service began its K9 (canine) program, since dogs can be very effective in sniffing out explosives. As do many agencies, the Secret Service primarily uses dogs from Holland called the Belgian Malanois. This breed is noted for its intelligence. Also, it has short hair, so it is easy for the dogs to work in the heat. Furthermore, it is a fast and friendly breed.

Each dog is trained while still a puppy before being matched with a handler. Then both the dog and handler go through twenty weeks of intense training specifically for Secret Service work. Even after this, each dog retrains eight hours every week for the rest of its career.

The dogs of the Secret Service's K9 team work and live with their handlers, who are uniformed officers, twenty-four hours a day. They form an intensely close bond. Most dogs retire when they are about ten years old. When a dog retires, it continues to live with its handler.

When training to be a member of the Secret Service, mastery of key equipment is paramount, including the portable metal detectors used at various sites.

I want to make sure if I'm going through a door with you, that I can trust you. If not, I'm not going to let you take that walk on graduation day.

Instructors like Mixon will not make your life at the Rowley Training Center easy. As you'd expect, they specifically design their classes to weed out anyone who is not capable of becoming a special agent or uniformed officer. It's never a pleasant task for the training center instructors to tell someone to leave, but it's sometimes necessary.

On the other hand, if you do make it through, you'll be ready for a proud moment: that "walk on graduation day," as Mixon called it. The graduation ceremony is a moving and exciting event, one that is often attended by the first lady or even the president as a way to acknowledge the importance of the Secret Service and its newly minted agents.

SUPPORT PERSONNEL TRAINING

Of course, only a handful of applicants to the Secret Service will be able to go through the training process and graduate as a new special agent or uniformed officer. The majority of people newly hired for the agency will be part of the large support staff that the USSS needs to keep operating on a daily basis. These employees are the nuts and bolts of the operation, making sure that all of the special agents and officers are able to do their jobs effectively and efficiently.

The training for a specific support job only takes a few days or a week of training. In some cases, you may even be able to learn everything you need to know while you are already on the job. In any case, you will be ready to become part of one of the most interesting branches of the entire U.S. law enforcement system.

If you've just become a new special agent or uniformed officer, you'll be ready for your first assignment. If you're a newly minted special agent, you'll be assigned to one of the USSS's field offices across the country, the agency's headquarters in Washington, D.C., or one of its overseas offices in several cities, including Paris, London, Bonn, Rome, or Bangkok.

The same is true if you're on the way to being a support employee. Naturally, you'll go where someone with your particular skills is needed at the time. But if you've just become a uniformed officer, you'll be assigned to a position in one of the many locations the agency maintains around the White House and other key government buildings.

Typically, special agents spend their first six to eight years of service assigned to a field office. Typically, this assignment will pair you with senior agents who will mentor you and help you learn the ropes of your new job. Often, an agent's first experiences are with a fraud or anti-counterfeiting team.

After this, the next step in your career typically involves a transfer to a protective detail. In part because the Secret Service doesn't want its agents to burn out from the pressures of this job, you will probably stay there for only three to five years before being rotated out. Following their stints in protective detail, agents generally return to the field or transfer to an assignment in the Washington, D.C. area. This could be at the Secret Service's headquarters, to Rowley Training Center for a position as an instructor, or some other D.C.-based assignment.

At some point in your career, you may have the opportunity to work overseas in one of the agency's international field offices. As you'd expect, this typically requires extra training, particularly language training, to ensure that you can work alongside the Secret Service's foreign law enforcement counterparts.

FOUR

ON THE JOB

SINCE SPECIAL AGENTS AND UNIFORMED OFFICERS have so many different aspects to their work, no two days on the job are alike. In fact, any sworn officer will tell you that this variety is one of the most appealing aspects of the job. Every day can also present a fresh challenge for the service's support personnel. One thing is guaranteed: a job with the Secret Service is never boring.

SETTING UP SECURITY

While special agents are best known for trotting alongside the presidential limousine and otherwise directly body guarding their protectees, some of the most important part of protective work happens elsewhere. This work is preventative—that is, work done on an ongoing basis, or just before an event, to ensure safety.

An important part of the Secret Service agents' work is the preparation and securing of a site before the President arrives.

For example, the service maintains files on roughly 40,000 U.S. citizens who have been identified as possible threats. The vast majority of these people are not considered serious risks, but the Secret Service nonetheless maintains files on them just in case. It keeps closer tabs on anyone who may present a serious and specific hazard. In that case, agents will regularly interview them and those around them to assess how genuine the danger might be. If the agents determine that there is a high risk, they will step up their watch on the individual.

The agency is also responsible for site advance and protecting the environment whenever a protectee makes a public appearance. This involves inspecting the location ahead of time and planning how to carry out protective action if needed.

For example, ten days before a presidential trip, at least eight to twelve agents fly to the destination. Joining them are as many counter-snipers and other specialists as needed. They look for any security weaknesses there and create a plan, including such factors as establishing checkpoints, creating emergency evacuation routes, and establishing bases at local hospitals.

These preparations are very thorough. Agents sweep offices and hotel rooms for bugs, measure the environment's air quality to check for dangerous bacteria, and test food that their charges will be eating by watching while food is being prepared, then selecting dishes at random to test when they are served. The agency even requires that any kitchen employee who has been convicted of a serious crime be given the day off.

Protecting the environment is what happens during the event. Agents patrol the grounds and stay close to their protectees, keep in touch via a temporary command post. Then, after the event, agents analyze the operation, studying ways to improve future procedures.

All of this preparation is elaborate and painstaking. It may at times feel like overkill—that is, agents go too far to prepare for contingencies. However, it is vital to the success of an operation. Chief of Staff Pierson remarks, "If we can protect the environment, we can protect everyone within that environment."

WORKING THE ROPE LINE

Meanwhile, when a protectee makes a public appearance, the service's work is more visible. Details vary, but some aspects are standard for any public appearance. For example, according to Robert Rodriguez, a retired special agent, this team typically guards a presidential candidate:

> The standard protection is at least two details on the campaign trail, sometimes a third. They rotate every three weeks. There will be considerably more protection [as candidates begin] moving into the general election. The Secret Service will start to provide countersniper teams, counterassault teams, magnetometer teams, K9 units and countersurveillance units, for example.

Especially dangerous moments come when protectees are "working the rope line"—that is, as they reach into crowds to shake hands. (The name comes from the ropes that once kept crowds from surging too close. Today, this cordon is typically a metal barrier.) In this case, agents are stationed on both sides of the barrier.

For obvious reasons, the protectee is especially vulnerable to attack at such times. Safety considerations must be balanced against the wishes of the protectee to connect with the public. Retired Assistant Special Agent Bruce Bowen remarks, "We're sometimes at the center of opposing philosophies. We would prefer to keep the president in a glass bubble for four or eight years. The [White House] staff wants to have maximum exposure. It's our duty to reach a happy medium."

Secret Service agents typically dislike the rope line, because of their protectee's vulnerability, but the protectee

A DAY IN THE LIFE

Some of a special agent's work may seem dull, such as waiting around in hotel rooms while dignitaries get ready for a public appearance. Even then, however, agents must remain vigilant, so it is impossible for them to slack off while on duty.

Besides, overall, the life of a special agent is hardly dull. In fact, one of the most appealing aspects of working in the Secret Service is the variety it offers. Julia Pierson, a former special agent who is now the service's Chief of Staff, describes a typical schedule:

In the field offices, you're doing interviews or meeting with the U.S. Attorney in the morning, and meeting with a victim or criminal in the afternoon. In the evening, you might go to a briefing about a protective visit the next day. Our field agents have the most variety in terms of doing a little bit of everything. It's about 50-50 investigation and protection.

In protective operations, there are three shifts: day, evening and midnight. The interesting thing about protection is that when you're traveling, the clock is changing, and your shift can get extended. Even just the logistics of trying to get a relief team to you can extend your shift. You're pretty much responsible for the whole duration of the trip.

One day you can be on a protective assignment, staying in a plush hotel, with an interesting political theme, whether it's a convention or a campaign or other significant world event. And then the following week you could be serving a search warrant on a criminal element related to a financial-fraud investigation. I joke all the time that we train our agents to have a little bit of an attention deficit disorder. There isn't any task that I could assign that couldn't be done in a two-week time frame. . . .

Perhaps the biggest downside is juggling your personal life. [When] we're getting prepared for the [next presidential] campaign . . . agents will spend twenty-one days out, come back for twenty-one and then go out again. These trips can be very exciting and interesting, but life continues to happen around them. If you have a sick family member or other family matter, it can be very awkward to manage. And on protective assignments, you and the other agents are living with each other, traveling with each other, eating lunch with each other, spending your lives with each other. It can be challenging.

Source: Siobhan Roth, "For Hire: Secret Service Agent," Smithsonian.com, June 01, 2007, www.smithsonianmag.com/people-places/forhire_secret.html

probably also doesn't like it much. *Newsweek* writer Katie Paul comments, "How would you feel if a frowning man in dark sunglasses and wires in his ears grabbed the back of your pants every time you walked into a crowd?"

Although a protectee's day is usually tightly scheduled, sometimes the unexpected happens. In such cases, the service's "jump teams" go into action—for example, when Nicolas Sarkozy, the president of France, made an unplanned jog through completely unsecured Central Park while visiting New York City.

WHAT THE WELL-DRESSED SPECIAL AGENT WEARS

While on protective duty, Secret Service agents carry tools such as standard firearms and handcuffs, and they wear bullet-resistant vests. Agents are also frequently seen wearing sunglasses. These are not required, but they are popular for a variety of reasons: because they cut the glare of sunlight, making it easier for agents to scan crowds; to keep crowds from noticing which way the agents are looking; and to protect their eyes in case of trouble.

Just as sunglasses are not required, there is no formal dress code for special agents. However, they typically wear clothes that are appropriate for the occasion. Most circumstances call for a conservative suit, but their dress can also range from blue jeans for informal occasions to tuxedos or formal gowns when on duty at state dinners or on other fancy occasions.

In addition to their other gear, agents famously wear earpieces with cords trailing into their collars. These are part of a complex communications system headquartered in a command center. This system ensures that all agents on duty are aware of important information, such as the protectee's location and when the next phase of an operation occurs.

Another part of an agent's communication equipment is the small microphone he or she wears near the wrist. When you see agents appearing to talk into their sleeves, that's exactly what they are doing.

NOT ALL GLAMOUR AND EXCITEMENT

Being on protective duty is a high-pressure job with more than its share of fast-moving action. However, the job isn't always an exciting adrenaline rush. Secret Service agents also spend a lot of time guarding their charges during non-public times—which can mean, essentially, just waiting around. Retired special agent Dennis McCarthy comments, "For all the glamour and excitement, there are countless hours of standing alone in deserted hotel corridors outside a door behind which the president is sleeping."

Meanwhile, some of the jobs required of special agents on protective duty are, to say the least, unusual. Take the experience of one of the agents assigned to shield President Jimmy Carter's daughter, Amy.

While Amy was attending an elaborate pet show on an estate in Virginia, a three-ton elephant escaped from its handlers and charged the audience. The creature got within about thirty-five feet (10.6 m) of the first daughter before a special agent scooped her into his arms.

The agent quickly jumped over a split-rail fence, not long before the elephant crashed into the barrier and destroyed it. Amy was taken to safety inside the estate's main house as the rest of the crowd scattered and trainers struggled to control the rogue elephant.

COUNTERFEITING

Naturally, protecting key government officials and their families from harm is not the only job you'll do if you become a special agent. About half of the Secret Service's staff at any given moment is devoted to its original mandates—investigating and stopping counterfeiting, and otherwise protecting the nation's economic wellbeing. The service's investigative agents and support personnel make roughly three thousand arrests each year.

Since agents typically rotate in and out of various duties, you almost certainly will be assigned at some point to one of the USSS's anti-counterfeiting investigative teams. In fact, new agents often receive this posting as their first assignment, typically on a check-fraud team. Robert Sica, the deputy special agent in charge of the service's New York City field office, comments,

We can't have agents standing post [on protective duty] all year. The investigations are what keep the agents' minds sharp, which reinforces their effectiveness on protective details. The best protective agents are often the smartest ones, because they know how to read people. That comes from investigations.

To agents who are on financial investigative duty, "counterfeiting" means more than just creating false money. Phony identification papers and other documents, for instance, are other common targets for forgers. Nonetheless, the creation of "funny money" is still by far the counterfeiting crime that the agency most frequently investigates.

It's a big job. An estimated 200 million U.S. dollars in circulation today are counterfeit. While this is only a small fraction of the 500 billion dollars in total at any given time, it is still significant.

Counterfeiting money has changed significantly over the years, making the Secret Service's job both easier and more difficult. On the one hand, it is much harder for counterfeiters to make copies of money that are good enough to withstand close inspection. This is because the U.S. government regularly finds new ways to make currency that is difficult to reproduce. For example, bills are now printed on hard-to-match cotton fiber, not paper made from wood. New bills also have sophisticated security features built into them, such as holographic ribbons that change their appearance depending on how the bill is tilted.

On the other hand, the methods that criminals use to counterfeit money are also much more sophisticated. Computers, scanners, and other forms of technology have made it possible to easily reproduce currency that, in certain circumstances, looks real enough to be accepted as genuine. Brian L. Stafford, a retired director of the Secret Service, comments, "We have seen a reinvention of how a counterfeit is made. Before, you needed skilled [artists] to make a passable counterfeit. Today we have children doing it."

CHASING PHONY MONEY

Another factor in catching counterfeiters is that a considerable amount of phony money is printed and used not in America, but overseas. For example, U.S. currency is generally considered desirable, so it is often used for deals among drug or arms smugglers in other countries.

Naturally, the temptation to use counterfeit bills for these deals is powerful. Furthermore, at least a portion of this counterfeit money is regularly smuggled into the U.S. Anthony M. Chapa, a retired special agent, commented in 1994,

> This has grown into an international crime that has no boundaries. The tentacles are around the world. The same [people] who produce counterfeits that show up in Los Angeles produce the counterfeits that are being passed in Madrid, Spain, or Quito, Ecuador.

Because of this international traffic, Secret Service anti-counterfeiting teams frequently collaborate with their colleagues overseas. If you are assigned to an anti-counterfeiting team, this may give you an opportunity to travel to or even be stationed in another country.

Or you may be assigned to another aspect of the Secret Service's anti-counterfeiting work: helping educate the public on spotting phony bills. This is important work, because bad money can be difficult for ordinary citizens to recognize.

Much of the counterfeit money in circulation today is good enough to pass in a quick transaction, especially in busy locations such as convenience stores or fast food restaurants. A big part of the Secret Service's job, then, is to show merchants how to spot phony money—and what to do about it. Retired director Stafford says, "Counterfeit currency is a real problem for [businesses]. If they accept a fake $100 bill, they can't exchange it for a real one."

THE UNIFORMED DIVISION

Complementing the counterfeiting and protective work of the Secret Service's special agents is the second main category of the agency's sworn officers. This is the Uniformed Division. As of 2011, there were more than 1,300 uniformed officers in this division.

If you have had little or no law enforcement experience, your best chance to join the Secret Service as a sworn officer will be through the Uniformed Division. In contrast to special agents, entry-level uniformed officers do not need extensive work experience.

In many ways, the Uniformed Division is a kind of super-police force. On the surface, it has many of the characteristics of a typical police department. For one thing, its ranks and titles are similar to those you'd find in a police department: officer, sergeant, lieutenant, captain, inspector, deputy chief, assistant chief, and chief. And then there are the uniforms, which resemble those of typical regional law enforcement agencies.

Beyond these surface similarities, however, the Uniformed Division is hardly your typical police force. Its primary responsibility is to protect the White House and other key government buildings. Among these other buildings are the main Treasury Building, the official residence of the vice president, and foreign diplomatic missions in the Washington, D.C. area.

It's a job that requires people with sharp eyes, ears, and brains. According to one source, at least one unauthorized person tries to get into the White House every day, not posing a genuine threat but simply hoping to talk to the president. An average of two a month, meanwhile, try to ram the White House gates in cars, scale the eight-foot-high fences around the compound, or otherwise create violent disruptions. And that's not even counting the many attempted breaches of security at any of the other buildings the Uniformed Division patrols.

To cover the areas it protects, the Uniformed Division has established a network of permanent security posts. You might be assigned to staff one of these posts. You may also be assigned to one of the Uniformed Division's mobile teams. These teams patrol their areas on foot, by bicycle, and in motor vehicles. In addition, they make use of a broad array of surveillance devices, from cameras with 24/7 monitoring and alarms to other security devices that the Secret Service keep highly classified.

CLEARING THE WAY

In this passage, journalist Marc Ambinder describes the kinds of procedures the Secret Service takes in preparation for a General Assembly of the United Nations in New York City:

Large events such as the General Assembly pose particular hurdles...

Every venue to be used must be cleared by the Technical Security Division. First, 130 dog teams, many borrowed from other agencies, sniff for explosives. Then agents conduct fire-safety surveys; coordinate the placement of chemical, biological, and radiological sensors; and, for some rooms, add bulletproof glass and blast webbing to the windows.

This year [2011], housing agents faced an additional threat to national security: bedbugs. It would have been an obvious embarrassment if any of the General Assembly protectees had been bitten by the pests that have of late plagued New York City. None were, but one agent wasn't so lucky. As a gag, fellow agents posted his injured-in-the-line-of-duty portrait on a wall in one of the temporary offices leased by the service.

Source: Marc Ambinder, "Inside the Secret Service," Atlantic.com, March 2011, www.theatlantic.com/magazine/archive/2011/03/inside-the-secret-service/8390/

If you join the uniformed division of the Secret Service, there's an excellent chance you'll be patrolling key government buildings.

It is likely that you might join one of the group's several specialized units that are organized within the Uniformed Division. These include:

The Countersniper Support Unit, which defends against sniper fire. If you visit the White House or attend a presidential event, you might see armed men on the roof. These are members of the countersniper unit. Since the unit was founded in 1971, its members have yet to fire a single shot on duty.

As a countersniper, your presence will hardly be a secret, although the specifics of your job, naturally, will be confidential. CNN reporters Jeanne Meserve and Mike M. Ahlers comment,

> The Secret Service doesn't mind you knowing they are up there. In fact, their mere presence at the

The Secret Service has a countersniper team that constantly surveys public gatherings for any potential snipers.

inauguration has a deterrent effect, they say. But they are mum about many other details, including how many teams will be deployed, how long they work and about their custom firearms. Unit commander Lt. Bernard Hall jokingly calls the weapon [they use] a JAR—"Just Another Rifle."

The Canine (K9) Explosive Detection Team pairs specially trained dogs with handlers to sniff out explosives. Formed in 1976, this team is deployed to protect all of the locations and individuals who are guarded by the Secret Service.

If you join the Canine Explosive Detection Team, you and your four-legged partner will train at the Secret Service facility in Maryland. You'll be based in Washington, D.C., but will

The Canine Explosive Detection team uses dogs that have been specifically trained to sniff out explosives.

frequently travel across the country as needed. (As with so much else about the service, the exact number of its canine teams and other details are classified.)

The Emergency Response Team, which was founded in 1992 and focuses specifically on stopping unauthorized entry to the White House grounds. These heavily armed officers are "[d]ressed head to toe in black . . . skilled, unobtrusive and absolutely lethal when called upon," Niall Firth of the Daily Mail (U.K.) commented in an article on the team.

In the course of their work, team members have stopped a variety of would-be intruders, ranging from "fence jumpers" to a man who crashed a light airplane into the residence in 1994. (President Bill Clinton and his family were not there at the time. The pilot was killed in the crash.)

The Magnetometer Team, which operates the magnetometers (metal detectors) at all environments where the Secret Service is responsible for security. This branch of the Uniformed Division was formed following the attempted assassination of President Reagan in 1981.

Many of the metal detector stations you might be assigned to as a member of this team are permanent fixtures in key government buildings. At one time, portable magnetometers were also used for all public events where there was a Secret Service presence. However, controversially, portable machines have sometimes not been employed at these occasions, because using them slows down the process of seating guests significantly.

SUPPORT POSITIONS

As in any law enforcement agency, the sworn officers of the Secret Service—that is, its special agents and uniformed officers rely on a wide range of support personnel, ranging from technical and specialized positions to administrative jobs. The USSS is no exception.

Daily life as one of the agency's support personnel, as you can imagine, can vary widely. You may be stationed at the agency's D.C. headquarters, or at any of its field offices or overseas offices. And, of course, your daily life will no doubt be a busy one, with a constant series of tasks arising to challenge you.

TIPS ON DETECTING COUNTERFEIT BILLS

If you get money that you think is phony, look at it. Compare it to a genuine note of the same denomination and series. Look for differences, not similarities.

The portrait should be lifelike and should stand out distinctly from the background. Counterfeit portraits are generally lifeless, flat, and not well detailed.

The lines of the border should be clear and unbroken.

Genuine serial numbers are evenly spaced. They are printed the same color as the Treasury Seal. Also, the numbers should be uniformly spaced.

The paper should have tiny red and blue fibers in it. Sometimes counterfeiters try to simulate this with tiny printed red and blue lines. Real notes have the lines embedded in the paper, not on the surface.

If you find money that you think might be counterfeit:

- Don't give it back to the person who passed it to you.
- If you can, delay the passer. Observe him or her, and try to get a license plate number if the passer uses a car. Remember what the passer and any companions look like.
- Contact your local police department or Secret Service field office.
- Write your initials and the date in the white border areas of the suspect note.
- Try not to handle the note too much. Carefully put it in a clean, protective covering, such as an envelope.
- Give it to only a properly identified police officer or Secret Service special agent.

Some of these jobs are categorized as technical specialties, such as:
- document analysis
- chemistry
- engineering
- fingerprint analysis
- forensic photography

Others are administrative and management specialties, including:
- financial management
- human resources
- recordkeeping and database management
- office management
- media relations
- accountancy
- policy and law

And there are many other support positions as well, such as:
- intelligence research and analysis
- polygraph operation
- psychology
- social work
- information technology
- surveillance technology
- telecommunications
- facilities management

- mechanical, building, weapons, and vehicle fleet maintenance
- investigation assistance

RESEARCH AND INTELLIGENCE SPECIALISTS

One example of a position that may appeal to you is that of a Criminal Research Specialist. Criminal Research Specialists gather, analyze, and present information that may help agents, uniformed officers, and technical personnel do their jobs better. The job makes frequent and extensive use of computer databases, electronic spreadsheets, desktop publishing, mapping software, and other professional tools.

The information you'll handle as a Criminal Research Specialist will have a major impact on active investigations, possible future investigations, research into crime trends, and the clearance of unresolved cases. You may also become part of a task force focusing on such issues as pinpointing the reasons behind mass killings at schools, or developing psychological profiles of potential assassins. Other task forces concentrate on specific cases, such as threats against a public figure that must be traced back to the responsible parties. Richard Elias, the deputy assistant director of the Secret Service, remarks, "If a threat is made against the President, we want to know it. Whether it's a drunk in a bar or an identified terrorist, we're going to investigate it."

You might also consider becoming an Intelligence Research Assistant. In this job, you will support senior members of the USSS's Protective Intelligence and Assessment Division, which is devoted to gathering, analyzing, and reporting on intelligence that concerns its protective duties.

Your responsibilities as an Intelligence Research Assistant will include preparing intelligence information; handling data across various automated systems; starting and maintaining records and database systems; establishing trip folders and computer records for work-related trips within the United States; and maintaining other intelligence and law enforcement administrative files.

Research and intelligence jobs such as these are clearly vital to the Secret Service's missions. The primary goal of these missions, of course, is to prevent bad incidents from ever taking place—so every operation begins with extensive research and an intelligence assessment. Your job will thus include tasks such as gathering information (from virtually every part of the intelligence community in the U.S. and elsewhere) and preparing detailed profiles of protectees, including information on any potential enemy.

FORENSIC SPECIALISTS

Another vital support area you might want to be part of is forensic science. The bulk of the Secret Service's forensic work is carried out at its laboratory in Washington, D.C. The specialists assigned there analyze and report on pieces of evidence such as suspicious documents, fingerprints, false identification, credit cards, or currency.

Within the general category of forensic science, you will have more specific responsibilities and tasks. These include

Forensic officers can often secure an arrest and conviction in important cases with the evidence they obtain at crime scenes.

such jobs as recording and coordinating photographic and graphic evidence; providing video, audio, and image enhancement services (such as making surveillance audiotapes easier to understand); providing expert testimony in court cases; and creating visual and 3-D modeling and simulation tools to help in situations such as training exercises and court testimony.

One crucial aspect of the USSS's forensic lab is its International Ink Library. With over 10,000 digitized samples, this database is the largest of its kind in the world. The information in this bank is valuable because the ink used to write a threatening document, forged currency, or other printed items is often an important clue to locating the document's origin. As a Secret Service ink specialist, you will analyze an ink sample's "fingerprint" and, by using the information already in the library, pinpoint such information as its brand, composition, and the date when it was first manufactured. This, in turn, will help the Secret Service's special agents in their pursuit of criminals.

The USSS's ink library has proved invaluable in countless criminal investigations. According to FRTech, the newsletter of the Department of Homeland Security's First Responder Technologies Program, "The International Ink Library has helped investigate forged documents, threats against government officials, suspected terrorism, child pornography and missing or exploited children, medical fraud, war crimes, and obstruction of justice cases."

Clearly, many aspects of the Secret Service's job openings will offer you the possibility of having an interesting, fast-moving, and varied career. Even if you don't become a special agent or a uniformed officer, there are plenty of other options. Depending on your interests and skills, you might become, for instance, an expert in high-tech surveillance, a forensic photographer, a psychologist who helps evaluate the profiles of people who make potentially dangerous threats, or a weapons specialist who keeps the service's firearms in top shape. The choice is yours.

FIVE

BENEFITS AND
SALARIES

ALL OF THE MANY CAREERS WITHIN THE SECRET
Service, for support employees and sworn officers alike, come
with one important built-in benefit: the satisfaction of a job
well done, a job that carries with it the knowledge that you're
helping to protect some of the world's most important government figures and keeping the country's economic structure safe.

On the other hand, personal satisfaction is obviously not
enough. Everyone needs more than that to live. Even with the
most personally satisfying job in the world, you'll still need to
eat and have a home.

So, like any other large organization, the Secret Service
offers its employees a variety of compensation packages that
include pay, health insurance, and many other benefits. And
since the service is part of the federal government, all of those
pay and benefits packages are generous.

SALARIES FOR SPECIAL AGENTS AND UNIFORMED OFFICERS

As a federal employee, your pay and benefits will be set according to guidelines that have been established for anyone who works for the federal government. In the case of special agents, uniformed officers, and specialists, salaries are based on a standardized plan called the General Schedule (GS).

The GS has fifteen pay grades, and within each grade are ten steps. These are adjusted every year for inflation (that is, they rise to reflect changes in the cost of living). The grades are referred to as "GS-1," "GS-2," and so on. Each of the grades and the steps within them indicate specific salary levels. The level you begin at will depend on the job and various other factors, including your experience and education.

Then, as you rise in seniority and promotion, your place on the scale will rise and your salary will rise accordingly. Typically, federal employees, including those in the Secret Service, move up a pay grade after two or three years on the job. A move up the scale is determined by a variety of factors. Among them are the level of responsibility you have and the difficulty of your specific job.

Another factor in determining your salary will be seniority—that is, the number of years you have spent on the job. Still another factor is the quality of your performance evaluations. Performance evaluations are "report cards" that are prepared on a regular basis for employees. Your supervisor will prepare your evaluation, based in large part on how he or she judges how well you have done your work.

For some Secret Service employees, other factors are also considered. For instance, you may be eligible for extra pay if you are assigned to certain offices where the cost of living is higher.

Also, when determining salaries for special agents and uniformed officers, the government takes into consideration the potential dangers of the job. Agents and uniformed officers may be eligible to receive special, one-time bonuses of hazard pay for specific assignments. Overall, specific salary rates for sworn officers in the federal government are determined by a modified version of the General Schedule. This is called the GL or GL-LEO (for "law enforcement officer"). Other specific jobs come with salaries that are also determined by modified versions of the basic schedule. For example, the pay for scientific specialists is determined by the GST schedule.

To see current pay grades and learn more about the General Schedule and the government's policies concerning salaries for federal employees, you can visit the U.S. Office of Personnel Management's website: www.opm.gov/oca/11tables/index.asp.

SALARIES FOR UNIFORMED OFFICERS

If you are a newly graduated sworn officer, you will enter the government pay system after finishing your months at the Rowley Training Center and assignment to your first field office position. (Your expenses will be covered while you are at Rowley.)

The exact pay grade for your first years on the job will depend on factors such as your qualifications and education.

For example, special agents are typically hired at the GL-7 level. As of 2011, the lowest base salary in this grade was $43,964.

However, your base salary is just that: a base. Again depending on your qualifications and education, as well as factors such as the location of your first assignment, your salary range can be much higher. For example, a starting special agent in 2011 could earn as much as $74,891. If you choose to remain with the service and rise to a senior management level, your salary will increase quite a bit. As of 2011, salaries for Secret Service employees at higher management-level positions often reached well over $100,000. Positions at these higher levels are typically supervisory jobs—that is, overseeing the work of field agents and support staff.

In addition to the salary you receive according to the General Schedule, special agents and uniformed officers are eligible to receive a form of extra pay called Law Enforcement Availability Pay (LEAP). This pay is given to all federal law enforcement officers who are criminal investigators. For the Secret Service, this bonus will be 25% of your regular salary.

Availability pay is a way of compensating you for just that— your availability. (Overtime pay is figured on a different scale.) The Secret Service recognizes that its special agents and uniformed officers do not hold down regular nine-to-five positions.

Officially, your regular schedule will be similar to a normal work schedule in a business—that is, a 40-hour week. However, in practice this is virtually never the case. As a special agent or uniformed officer, you'll be expected to work long hours, sometimes on weekends and at odd times that are quite

AN UNDESIRABLE BENEFIT

A benefit for its sworn agents that the Secret Service hopes not to have to use is its provision for helping agents who have been injured while on the job—much less the families of agents who are killed while on duty.

Fortunately, over the service's long history, only a few Secret Service personnel have been killed or injured while on duty. The most recent incident of a special agent shot on duty was that of Special Agent Tim McCarthy, who was shot (but not fatally) in 1981 when John Hinckley Jr., tried to assassinate President Ronald Reagan.

To minimize the possibility of one of its personnel being wounded or killed, the Secret Service requires that all agents undergo periodic training. For example, agents who are on protection detail, as well as those on the Countersniper Support Unit and Emergency Response Team, are required to regularly attend the Secret Service's academy for firearms requalification, drills such as simulated emergency scenarios, and various other classes, workshops, and refresher classes.

different from your normal schedule. Former special agent Charles Brewster comments, "We never work an eight-hour day. We always give it at least two hours more or more than that. Sometimes we get overwhelmed with the number of hours we're working, but we try to always make time for the important things in life."

SALARIES FOR SUPPORT STAFF

As might be expected, if you are hired to fill a support staff position, your pay will depend on the specific job. But the Secret Service's support staff members are divided into two general categories. (The same is true for all federal employees.)

If you are starting a career as a professional in a specialized position, such as a linguist, IT technician, intelligence researcher, or forensic scientist, you will be paid according to the federal General Schedule. For example, many new employees enter the service at the GS-5 or GS-6 level. As of early 2011, the salary range at these levels went from about $34,000 to about $49,000. However, some specialized positions enter at higher levels, and so the pay is much higher. For example, as of 2011 an Information Technology Specialist for the Secret Service was considered to be at the GS-13 level, and so had a base salary of about $75,000.

As with sworn officers and any other government job, advancement up the scale for support specialists depends on seniority, performance reviews, promotions, and other factors. Typically, a move up to a pay grade takes place after two or three years on the job.

Meanwhile, the system of payment is different for blue-collar federal employees. Traditionally (but not always) blue-collar jobs are jobs that pay hourly wages, rather than a yearly salary. An example of such a job would be that of a mechanic who helps keep the Secret Service's automotive fleet in shape.

The system used to determine pay for federal blue-collar employees is called the Federal Wage System (FWS). The FWS is designed to keep pay scales in a given position roughly equal in all parts of the country, and to make sure that the employees' salaries are competitive with those in the private sector. In other words, if you are a blue-collar employee of the federal government, you are assured of being paid roughly the same as what you could earn at the same job outside the government. For example, in 2011 an automotive mechanic for the Secret Service earned about $28.00 per hour.

BENEFITS

In addition to the salaries it offers, the Secret Service provides its full-time employees with a generous package of other benefits. Many of these are the same that are offered to all federal employees, such as life insurance plans, savings plans, repayment for travel expenses, and paid days off for national holidays such as New Year's Day and Independence Day.

One of the major benefits that the Secret Service offers all of its employees is a low-cost comprehensive health plan for those employees and their families. It also provides other major benefits, such as life insurance plans, savings plans to help employees invest their money wisely, and financial aid and other benefits for agents who are injured or disabled while on the job. Provisions are also made to compensate the families of employees who have been permanently disabled or killed in the line of duty.

Full-time Secret Service employees are also eligible for annual vacation leave and sick leave days. As is generally true in all work situations, the number of paid leave and sick leave days you receive will increase depending on how long you have worked for the agency.

The Secret Service also follows federal guidelines in providing a number of other benefits. These include being able to take up to twelve weeks of unpaid leave for such events as the birth of a child, a serious personal health problem, or caring for an ill family member. Furthermore, the agency also follows guidelines established by the Family and Medical Leave Act (FMLA). These regulations cover all federal government employees. Employees can to take up to twelve weeks of unpaid leave during any twelve-month period, typically for the birth and care of a newborn child or for other serious family-related medical situations.

Another benefit in working for the Secret Service is that the agency will try to accommodate you if you need to relocate for serious personal reasons. An example of this would be if you and your family were the only people available to care for an ill or elderly parent. In such a case, the Secret Service would work to grant you a "hardship transfer" to a field office close to your family member.

KNOW YOUR PRESIDENTIAL LIMOUSINE

- The current presidential limousines, the ones you see Secret Service agents running next to on the street, are one-of-a-kind Cadillacs built on modified truck chassis.

- The Secret Service will not reveal how many are available to the president, but it has been rumored that there are about a dozen. The current models are also rumored to be diesel-powered.

- It has been estimated that each limo costs about $300,000.

- The Secret Service refers to the presidential limousine as "Limo One" or "Cadillac One," but it is nicknamed "The Beast."

- Over the years, some presidents have ridden in Cadillacs, some in Lincolns.

- Each limo is equipped with features such as military-grade armor plating that is several inches thick and advanced communications equipment. It is modified so that it can be driven even if the tires have been shot out.

- The current limos are so heavy—an estimated 15,000 pounds (6803 kg)—that they use tires designed for medium- and heavy-duty trucks.

- President William McKinley, who was assassinated in 1901, was the first president to ride in an automobile. The first president to have an official, government-owned motorcar was his successor, Theodore Roosevelt. In 1939, Franklin Delano Roosevelt became the first president to have a specially built car for his use exclusively.

- In the 1940s, President Franklin Delano Roosevelt temporarily used a limo that had once belonged to gangster Al Capone while the official presidential vehicle was being renovated.

- In 2011, President Barack Obama was riding in one of his limos when it got stuck on a ramp as it left the U.S. Embassy in Dublin, Ireland. It was towed away as a huge crowd watched.

- The doors weigh about as much as the cabin doors on a Boeing 757.

- The thickness of the window glass lets very little natural light into the inside of the limo, so it is equipped with special interior lighting. It is essentially soundproof, although outside noises, of crowds, etc., can be piped in through speakers.

- It has its own oxygen supply, firefighting system, and blood bank.

- The presidential limo's door has no key. It is opened by Secret Service agents in a way that is highly classified. It can be locked like a bank vault if necessary.

- It seats seven. There is a small folding desk between the two rear seats.

- The limo is always driven by a highly trained Secret Service agent. Normally, the president's chief protective agent rides in front alongside the driver.

- When the limo is used overseas, the flag of the home nation replaces the United States flag that usually adorns it.

- It gets about eight miles to the gallon in fuel consumption.

Furthermore, the Secret Service, along with other federal agencies, has a system called a voluntary leave transfer program. This means that you can donate your unused annual leave days to other employees who have used all their available days off. This program is typically used when an employee needs extra time to recover from an injury or to care for a family member. That employee can "borrow" days off from colleagues to augment the standard amount of his or her leave.

Secret Service employees are eligible for a number of other, smaller benefits as well. For example, you may also be eligible for moving expenses when you are reassigned to a new location. Another example is a benefit you can claim if you are a special agent who is fluent in certain second languages. This is a one-time bonus given as a lump sum (that is, all at once) equal to 25 percent of your basic annual pay.

RETIREMENT

If you maintain your career with the Secret Service until retirement age, you'll be eligible for a number of other benefits. One of these is the service's pension plan. Generally, the amount of pension money you'll get after retirement depends on how many years of service you've given and how much you were paid.

Any employee with the Secret Service is eligible for retirement with a full pension at age fifty. There is no official cutoff age at which Secret Service employees must retire, except in the case of special agents and uniformed officers. These sworn

CONFIDENTIAL INFORMANTS

Sometimes, special agents on counterfeit detail use information they have received from confidential informants (CIs). As the phrase suggests, these are civilians who are enlisted to help the Secret Service in its investigations while remaining anonymous.

Employing informants during an investigation can be useful, even essential. The Secret Service has the legal right to use informants. However, it takes great care when doing so, in part because informants are often unreliable. Informants are usually paid for the information they provide, although this amount can vary widely.

For example, in 2010 it was revealed that a confidential informant used in cracking a massive credit-card theft scheme in Miami, Florida, was paid $75,000 a year. (The same informant was later given a twenty-year prison term for running a multi-million-dollar credit card scam of his own.) On the other hand, the Secret Service paid a former identity thief in Columbia, South Carolina, only about $18,000 a year during another undercover operation to catch card thieves.

With or without the help of a confidential informant, as a Secret Service anti-counterfeiting agent you will likely take part in sting operations to catch criminals. An example of such stings was an operation in northern New Jersey that ended in 2011.

It was put together when the Secret Service became aware of a gang that was passing bad money. These criminals made small purchases at stores like Target with large counterfeit bills, receiving real money as change. Over the course of several months, the crew passed thousands of dollars in bad money this way.

But stores in the area became suspicious, and their suspicions were confirmed when they realized that bills with the same serial numbers were being used in several different places. The Secret Service entered at that point, setting up a sting. An operative bought thousands of dollars in fake bills from the criminals, at a fraction of the value of real money.

The gang members were arrested and later convicted. Their crime was relatively small compared to other forgers—there have been cases where hundreds of thousands of dollars' worth of bad money was passed. But the New Jersey sting illustrates a key part of the Secret Service's work: a zero-tolerance policy. As the agency's website notes, "Each counterfeiting case, no matter how large or small, carries . . . serious consequences."

Source: "Counterfeit Awareness." Know Your Money, US Secret Service, www. secretservice.gov/money_technologies.shtml officers are required to retire at fifty-seven. However, they may be able to continue working for the service in other positions.

On the other hand, when you retire from the Secret Service, you may choose to take on another career outside of the agency. The skills and experience you have acquired in your career with the service will ensure that you will be in demand on the job market. For example, former special agents are often hired by local law enforcement agencies, as well as by other federal organizations such as the CIA, the U.S. Marshals Service, or the National Security Agency. Still other former special agents and retired employees choose to teach, go into law practice, or become private investigators or security consultants.

All in all, the salary and benefits that come with a career in the Secret Service make it a very attractive job choice. However, it is clear that there are many more—and better—reasons than just money to join the USSS. Interesting, fulfilling, and important work—that's what you'll find when you choose a career with the United States Secret Service.

GLOSSARY / NOTES

GLOSSARY

anarchist—A person who opposes formal governments

counterfeiting—The creation of false currency

magnetometer—A metal detector

protectees—Those under the official protection of the Secret Service

sworn officers—Law officers who have sworn official oaths of service and are authorized to carry firearms

NOTES

INTRODUCTION

p. 8, "His quick actions . . . ": Quoted in PBS Newshour, "Revisiting the Reagan Assassination Attempt, 30 Years Later," March 30, 2011, www.pbs.org/newshour/bb /white_house/jan-june11/reagan_03-30.html

p. 9, "We understand . . . ": Quoted in Laura Blumenfeld, "The Making of an Agent," *Washington Post*, July 26, 2009, www.washingtonpost.com/wp-dyn/content /article/2009/07/17/AR2009071701785_pf.html

p. 10, "It may be true . . . ": Marc Ambinder, "Inside the Secret Service," Atlantic.Com, March 2011, www.theatlantic.com/magazine/archive/2011/03 /inside-the-secret-service/8390/

p. 10-11., "[F]or many of you . . . ": Quoted in "Michelle Obama Visits US Department of Homeland Security 14 April 2009." www.dhs.gov/xlibrary/assets/michelle-obama-visits-department-04-apr-09.txt

CHAPTER 1

p. 12, "[W]hat we'll do . . . ": Quoted in Ronald Kessler, In the President's Secret Service, New York, Crown, 2009, p. 100

p. 14, "The chase . . . ": Quoted in Ronald Kessler, *In the President's Secret Service*, New York, Crown, 2009, p. 4

p. 16-17, "Secret Service men accompanied . . . ": "Appendix 7," Report of the President's Commission on the Assassination of President Kennedy, National Archives, www.archives.gov/research/jfk/warren-commission-report/appendix7.html

p. 17, "It took three . . . ": Joel Achenbach, "Inside the Secret Service, " *Washington Post*, July 9, 1993, http://www.washingtonpost.com/wp-srv/style/longterm/movies/features/dcmovies/secretservice.htm, retrieved June 7, 2011

p. 18, "Before the Kennedy assassination . . . ": Quoted in Ronald Kessler, *In the President's Secret Service*, New York, Crown, 2009, p. 112

p. 20, "While the question . . . ": Helene Cooper and Brian Stelter, "Obamas' Uninvited Guests Prompt an Inquiry," *New York Times*, November 26, 2009, www.nytimes.com/2009/11/27/us/politics/27party.html

p. 21, "People don't realize . . . ": Quoted in Siobhan Roth, "For Hire: Secret Service Agent," Smithsonian.com, June 01, 2007, www.smithsonianmag.com/people-places/forhire_secret.html

p. 25, "We're a small agency . . . ": Quoted in Siobhan Roth, "For Hire: Secret Service Agent," Smithsonian.com, June 01, 2007, www.smithsonianmag.com/people-places/forhire_secret.html

p. 27, "The men and women . . . ": Anonymous, "Support Personnel," secretservice.gov, www.secretservice.gov /whoweare_support.shtml

CHAPTER 2

p. 31, "Initially, I got involved . . . ": Quoted in Siobhan Roth, "For Hire: Secret Service Agent," Smithsonian.com, June 01, 2007, www.smithsonianmag.com/people-places /forhire_secret.html

p. 37, 39, "Whether you're an English major . . . ": Quoted in Siobhan Roth, "For Hire: Secret Service Agent," Smithsonian.com, June 01, 2007, www.smithsonianmag.com /people-places/forhire_secret.html

p. 39, "From day one . . . ": Christopher Reich, "They'd Take a Bullet For The President," Parade.com, www.parade.com/ news/2009/01/they-would-give-their-lives-for-the -president.html

p. 40, "I've flown all over . . . ": "Tracking Down Assassins and Counterfeiters: A Day in the Life of a Secret Service Agent," Lutheran Senior Services, http://lssliving.org /blog/2011/05/10/tracking-down-assassins-and-counter-feiters-a-day-in-the-life-of-a-secret-service-agent/

p. 45, "Yes, I encountered . . . ": Quoted in Ronald Kessler, *In the President's Secret Service*, New York, Crown, 2009, p. 99

p. 45, "You are always . . . ": Quoted in Ronald Kessler, *In the President's Secret Service*, New York, Crown, 2009, p. 99

p. 47, "We realize diversity . . . ": "Diversity and Inclusion," United States Secret Service, www.secretservice.gov/join /diversity.shtml

CHAPTER 3

p. 50, "Not all . . . ": Laura Blumenfeld, "The Making of an Agent." *Washington Post*, July 26, 2009, www.washington-post.com/wp-dyn/content/article/2009/07/17/AR2009071701785_pf.html

p. 53, "Everything we teach . . . ": Quoted in Ronald Kessler, *In the President's Secret Service*, New York, Crown, 2009, p. 105

p. 56, "You're attacked with guns . . . ": Quoted in Christopher Reich, "They'd Take a Bullet For The President," Parade. com, www.parade.com/news/2009/01/they-would-give-their-lives-for-the-president.html

p. 57, "Behind every mailbox . . . ": Laura Blumenfeld, "The Making of an Agent," *Washington Post*, July 26, 2009, www.washingtonpost.com/wp-dyn/content/article/2009/07/17/AR2009071701785_pf.html

p. 57, "We train . . . ": Quoted in Laura Blumenfeld, "The Making of an Agent," *Washington Post*, July 26, 2009, www.washingtonpost.com/wp-dyn/content/article/2009/07/17/AR2009071701785_pf.html

p. 58, "[D]ope dealers two blocks away . . . ": Quoted in Laura Blumenfeld, "The Making of an Agent," *Washington Post*, July 26, 2009, www.washingtonpost.com/wp-dyn/content/article/2009/07/17/AR2009071701785_pf.html

p. 58, "Don't forget to . . . "" Quoted in Laura Blumenfeld, "The Making of an Agent." *Washington Post*, July 26, 2009, www.washingtonpost.com/wp-dyn/content/article/2009/07/17/AR2009071701785_pf.html

p. 58, 60, "Details! . . . .": Quoted in Laura Blumenfeld, "The Making of an Agent," *Washington Post*, July 26, 2009, www.washingtonpost.com/wp-dyn/content /article/2009/07/17/AR2009071701785_pf.html

CHAPTER 4

p. 65, "If we can protect . . . ": Quoted in Siobhan Roth, "For Hire: Secret Service Agent," Smithsonian.com, June 01, 2007, www.smithsonianmag.com/people-places/forhire _secret.html

p. 66, "The standard protection . . . ": Quoted in Katherine Walsh, "The guarding of the president," Chief Security Officer, June 2008, http://books.google.com/books?id=c mAEAAAAMBAJ&pg=PT27&lpg=PT27&dq=secret+se rvice+%22rope+line%22&source=bl&ots=_9TrV3b2h5 &sig=0mGd4UA2LC9ItstttXsH1eAoSEM&hl=en&ei=7 usATv2AKuniiAKUq6CoCA&sa=X&oi=book_ result&ct=result&resnum=7&ved=0CE0Q6AEwBjgK #v=onepage&q=secret%20service%20%22rope%20 line%22&f=false

p. 66, "We're sometimes . . . ": Quoted in Marc Ambinder, "A Q And A On The President's Secret Service," *Atlantic*, November 29, 2009, www.theatlantic.com/politics /archive/2009/11/a-q-and-a-on-the-presidents-secret -service/30927/

p. 68, "How would you feel . . . ": Katie Paul, "Life With The Secret Service," *Newsweek*, November 13, 2008, www.newsweek.com/2008/11/12/life-with-the-secret- service.html

p. 69, "For all the glamour . . . ": Dennis McCarthy, *Protecting The President*, New York, New York: Dell, 1986, p. 7.

p. 70-71, "We can't have agents . . . ": Quoted in Marc Ambinder, "A Q and A On The President's Secret Service," *Atlantic*, November 29,2009, www.theatlantic.com /politics/archive/2009/11/a-q-and-a-on-the-presidents -secret-service/30927

p. 72, "We have seen a reinvention…" Quoted in Stefan Lovgren, "U.S. Secret Service's Other Job: Fighting Fake Money," *National Geographic*, October 22, 2004, http://news.nationalgeographic.com/news/2004/10 /1022_041022_tv_secret_service.html

p. 72, "This has grown into . . . ": Quoted in Stefan Lovgren, "U.S. Secret Service's Other Job: Fighting Fake Money," *National Geographic*, October 22, 2004, http://news .nationalgeographic.com/news/2004/10/1022_041022 _tv_secret_service.html

p. 73, "Counterfeit currency is a real problem…" Quoted in Stefan Lovgren, "U.S. Secret Service's Other Job: Fighting Fake Money," *National Geographic*, October 22, 2004, http://news.nationalgeographic.com/news/2004/10 /1022_041022_tv_secret_service.html

p. 76-77, "The Secret Service doesn't mind . . . ": Jeanne Meserve and Mike M. Ahlers, "Secret Service counter-snipers hunt for real snipers," CNN, January 19, 2009, http://articles.cnn.com/2009-01-19/us/sniper .training_1_secret-service-threat-countersniper-team? _s=PM:US

p. 78, "[d]ressed head to toe . . . ": Niall Firth, "Defending the White House," *Daily Mail (U.K.)*, December 16, 2010, www.dailymail.co.uk/sciencetech/article-1339147 /What-Obamas-White-House-Secret-Service-guard -wears-hes-protecting-him.html

p. 82, "If a threat is made . . . ": Quoted in Christopher Reich, "They'd Take a Bullet For The President," Parade.com, www.parade.com/news/2009/01/they-would-give-their -lives-for-the-president.html

p. 85, "The International Ink Library . . . ": "Analyzing Ink Spots," FRTech, June 2010, http://docs.google.com/viewer ?a=v&q=cache:ys1CmeQkye8J:www.firstresponder.gov /Pages/FRSiteCounts.aspx%3FSiteID%3D866+Secret+Se rvice's+forensic+laboratory.+%22+ink+library%22&hl= en&gl=us&pid=bl&srcid=ADGEEShEeXYIiWFQ5s7nB MMshCT9wGPIuZIiOLmCEY_WagVDl5ZbRdl8Qjf0hh 3NXl7nwzE5YLuFWAT16VSXD1tZDRL2xBU7rAiXR2I -VP0Neo1M16Owq3sAw65h1wqsvtyKPYU6JOb&sig=A HIEtbRoOYU2aUdI7X91QHuR9Lk2u8isnQ

CHAPTER 5

p. 91, "We never work . . . ": Quoted in Frosty Fowler, "Interview with Secret Service agent Charles Brewster," KGNW-AM Radio, April 19, 1997, http://cechambers. com/2011/06/11/frosty-fowlers-interview-with-secret- service-agent-charles-brewster/

FURTHER INFORMATION

BOOKS:

Bonanasinga, Jay, *Pinkerton's War: The Civil War's Greatest Spy and the Birth of the U.S. Secret Service*. Guilford, CT: Lyons Press, 2011.

Holden Henry, *To Be a U.S. Secret Service Agent*. Minneapolis, MN: Zenith Press, 2006.

Mitchell, Susan K., *The Secret World of Spy Agencies*. Berkeley Heights, NJ, Enslow, 2011.

Rooney, Anne, *Secret Services (Spies and Spying)*. Mankato, MN: Smart Apple Media, 2010.

Ryan, Jr., Bernard, *The Secret Service*. New York, NY: Chelsea House, 2010.

Wilber, Del Quinton, *Rawhide Down: The Near Assassination of Ronald Reagan*. New York, NY: Henry Holt, 2011.

WEBSITES

"United States Secret Service." secretservice.gov, www.secret service.gov

"The U.S. Secret Service Today," Inside the White House, clinton2.nara.gov, http://clinton2.nara.gov/WH/kids /inside/html/spring98-3.html

"U.S. Secret Service on Twitter," http://twitter.com /#!/SecretService

"U.S. Secret Service News," New York Times, http://topics. nytimes.com/topics/reference/timestopics /organizations/s/secret_service/index.html

"U.S. Secret Service News and Photos," Chicago Tribune, www.chicagotribune.com/topic/crime-law-justice/laws

/law-enforcement/u.s.-secret-service-ORGOV
0000126158.topic

BIBLIOGRAPHY

BOOKS

Andrew, Christopher, *For the President's Eyes Only: Secret Intelligence and the American Presidency from Washington to Bush.* New York, NY: HarperPerennial, 1995.

Kessler, Ronald, *In the President's Secret Service: Behind the Scenes with Agents in the Line of Fire and the Presidents they Protect.* New York, NY: Crown, 2009.

McCarthy, Dennis, *Protecting The President.* New York, New York: Dell, 1986.

Melanson, Philip H., *The Secret Service: The Hidden History of an Enigmatic Agency.* New York, NY: Carroll and Graf, 2002.

PERIODICALS AND WEBSITES:

Achenbach, Joel, "Inside the Secret Service," *Washington Post*, July 9, 1993, www.washingtonpost.com/wp-srv/style/longterm/movies/features/dcmovies/secretservice.htm

Ambinder, Marc, "Inside the Secret Service," Atlantic.com, March 2011, www.theatlantic.com/magazine/archive/2011/03/inside-the-secret-service/8390/

"Analyzing Ink Spots," FRTech, June 2010, http://docs.google.com/viewer?a=v&q=cache:ys1CmeQkye8J:www.firstresponder.gov/Pages/FRSiteCounts.aspx%3FSiteID%3D866+Secret+Service's+forensic+laboratory.+%22+ink

+library%22&hl=en&gl=us&pid=bl&srcid=ADGEEShE
eXYIiWFQ5s7nBMMshCT9wGPIuZIiOLmCEY
_WagVDl5ZbRdl8Qjf0hh3NXl7nwzE5YLuFWAT16VSX
D1tZDRL2xBU7rAiXR2I-VPM0Neo1M16Owq3sAw65h
1wqsvtyKPYU6JOb&sig=AHIEtbRoOYU2aUdI7X91QH
uR9Lk2u8isnQ

"Appendix 7," Report of the President's Commission on the
Assassination of President Kennedy. National Archives,
www.archives.gov/research/jfk/warren-commission
-report/appendix7.html

Blumenfeld, Laura, "The Making of an Agent," *Washington
Post*, July 26, 2009, www.washingtonpost.com/wp-dyn
/content/article/2009/07/17/AR2009071701785_pf.html

Cooper, Helene and Stelter, Brian, "Obamas' Uninvited
Guests Prompt an Inquiry," *New York Times*, November
26, 2009, www.nytimes.com/2009/11/27/us/politics
/27party.html

"Counterfeit Awareness: Know Your Money." U.S. Secret Service, secretservice.gov, www.secretservice.gov/money
_technologies.shtml

Firth, Niall, "Defending the White House," *Daily Mail (U.K.)*,
December 16, 2010, www.dailymail.co.uk/sciencetech
/article-1339147/What-Obamas-White-House-Secret
-Service-guard-wears-hes-protecting-him.html

Fowler, Frosty, "Interview with Secret Service agent Charles
Brewster," KGNW-AM Radio, April 19, 1997, http://
cechambers.com/2011/06/11/frosty-fowlers-interview
-with-secret-service-agent-charles-brewster/

Lovgren. Stefan, "U.S. Secret Service's Other Job: Fighting Fake Money," *National Geographic*, October 22, 2004, http://news.nationalgeographic.com/news/2004/10/1022 _041022_tv_secret_service.html

Meserve, Jeanne and Ahlers, Mike M., "Secret Service countersnipers hunt for real snipers," CNN, January 19, 2009, http://articles.cnn.com/2009-01-19/us/sniper.training_1 _secret-service-threat-countersniper-team?_s=PM:US

"Michelle Obama Visits US Department of Homeland Security 14 April 2009." Department of Homeland Security, dhs.gov, www.dhs.gov/xlibrary/assets/michelle-obama -visits-department-04-apr-09.txt

Paul, Katie, "Life With The Secret Service," *Newsweek*, November 13, 2008, www.newsweek.com/2008/11/12/ life-with-the-secret-service.html

PBS Newshour, "Revisiting the Reagan Assassination Attempt, 30 Years Later," pbs.org., March 30, 2011, www. pbs.org/newshour/bb/white_house/jan-june11/rea- gan_03-30.html

Reich, Christopher, "They'd Take a Bullet For The President," Parade.com, www.parade.com/news/2009/01/they -would-give-their-lives-for-the-president.html

Roth, Siobhan, "For Hire: Secret Service Agent," Smithsonian. com, June 01, 2007, www.smithsonianmag.com/people -places/forhire_secret.html

"Support Personnel." U.S. Secret Service, secretservice.gov, www.secretservice.gov/whoweare_support.shtml

"Tracking Down Assassins and Counterfeiters: A Day in the

Life of a Secret Service Agent." Lutheran Senior Services, lssliving.org, no date, http://lssliving.org/blog/2011/05/10 /tracking-down-assassins-and-counterfeiters-a-day-in -the-life-of-a-secret-service-agent/

Walsh, Katherine, "The guarding of the president," Chief Security Officer, June 2008, http://books.google.com /books?id=cmAEAAAAMBAJ&pg=PT27&lpg=PT27&d q=secret+service+%22rope+line%22&source=bl&ots= _9TrV3b2h5&sig=0mGd4UA2LC9ItstttXsH1eAoSEM& hl=en&ei=7usATv2AKuniiAKUq6CoCA&sa=X&oi=b ook_result&ct=result&resnum=7&ved=0CE0Q6AEwB jgK#v=onepage&q=secret%20service%20%22rope%20 line%22&f=false

INDEX

ABOUT THE AUTHOR

ADAM WOOG is the author of many books for adults, young adults, and children. His most recent books are *Military Might and Global Intervention* in the Controversy! series, and the five other titles in this series. Woog lives in his hometown of Seattle, Washington, with his wife. Their daughter, a college student, is majoring in criminal justice and criminology.